Echoes from the Margins:
Women's Travelogues and the Contested Colonial Landscape

Echoes from the Margins:
Women's Travelogues and the Contested Colonial Landscape

Ankita Mohanty
Gurudev Meher

BLACK EAGLE BOOKS
Dublin, USA | Bhubaneswar, India

Black Eagle Books
USA address:
7464 Wisdom Lane
Dublin, OH 43016

India address:
E/312, Trident Galaxy, Kalinga Nagar,
Bhubaneswar-751003, Odisha, India

E-mail: info@blackeaglebooks.org
Website: www.blackeaglebooks.org

First International Edition Published by
Black Eagle Books, 2025

ECHOES FROM THE MARGINS: WOMEN'S TRAVELOGUES AND THE CONTESTED COLONIAL LANDSCAPE
by Ankita Mohanty | Gurudev Meher

Copyright © **Ankita Mohanty | Gurudev Meher**

All rights reserved. No part of this publication may be reproduced, stored in a retrieval system, or transmitted, in any form or by any means, electronic, mechanical, photocopying, recording or otherwise without the prior permission of the publisher.

Cover & Interior Design: Ezy's Publication

ISBN- 978-1-64560-744-1 (Paperback)

Printed in the United States of America

Women are like tea bags. You never know how strong they are until they get into hot water.
—***Eleanor Roosevelt***

CONTENTS

Preface	09
Introduction	13
Chapter-I The Search for Identity through Travelogues	59
Chapter-II Emergence of Women Travel Writings	73
Chapter-III Travel Writing as Semi-Autobiographical Novel	83
Chapter-IV Misleading Titles	93
Chapter-V Travel Writing for Women Empowerment	111
Chapter-VI Women's Travel Writing as Resistance and Cultural Translation	134
Conclusion	141
Works Cited	158

Preface

Travel writing pulses as both a raw archive of human reckoning and a searing mirror of shifting power, identity, and culture. For centuries, its pages were claimed by male explorers, naturalists, and colonial administrators who stamped the world with an imperial, patriarchal gaze. In that shadowed terrain, women's travelogues emerge not as mere side notes but as acts of fierce resistance, self-invention, and radical testimony. This study ignites two such 19th-century texts: *A Princess's Pilgrimage* by Nawab Sikander Begum and *Wanderings of a Pilgrim in Search of the Picturesque* by Fanny Parkes. Though born from vastly different crossroads—one by a Muslim monarch under colonial India's yoke, the other by a British expatriate submerged in imperial currents—both works converge in their relentless drive to redraw the map of experience with a defiantly female pen.

Fanny Parkes plunged into colonial India not just as a visitor but as a metamorphosing force. Her wanderings erupt with ethnographic clarity and aesthetic fervour, wielding the 'picturesque' as a sharp tool to dissect cultural otherness. Yet she refuses the detached lens of the typical colonial voyeur. Slipping behind the veils of the zenana, she rips open the private lives of Indian women, translating their rituals, confidences, and griefs in a language of embodied intimacy. In that forbidden realm, Parkes stakes her claim: she writes from within, destabilizing the monolithic portrait of the colonized 'other' with every bold observation.

Nawab Sikander Begum's pilgrimage to Mecca and Medina unfolds as a royal manifesto disguised as a spiritual odyssey. Under the watchful glare of the British Raj, she seizes the act of writing in English—via a colonial intermediary—as an act of subversive sovereignty. Her narrative slashes through bureaucratic blunders in the Hijaz, interrogates Arabian social mores, and weaves together piety and reformist zeal. A ruler operating on the fringes of empire, she balances on a razor's edge: constrained by religion, gender, and colonial subjugation, yet speaking with unshakable moral force. Every candid critique, every prayerful reflection, reverberates with acute political consciousness.

Together, these travelogues shatter the binaries that uphold colonial discourse—insider versus outsider, observer versus observed, subject versus object. Parkes remakes her identity through total immersion; Begum cements hers through strategic authorship. Parkes enjoys the spoils of empire even as her prose trembles with unease at its arrogance. Begum couches her dissent in syntax palatable to British temperament, yet never surrenders her regal perspective. Positioned at opposite poles of the colonial spectrum, they both illuminate the brutal alchemy of power, gender, and authenticity forged in the crucible of travel.

Deploying feminist literary theory, postcolonial critique, and travel studies, this book rips open the layered politics inscribed in these texts. It reveals that these travelogues are not passive recollections or sterile geographic logs; they are battlegrounds where belonging, agency, and authorship are claimed—and violently defended. In these semi-autobiographical chronicles, Parkes and Begum invent new selves, staking out spaces that a world hell-bent on confining them never intended to grant.

By juxtaposing *A Princess's Pilgrimage* and *Wanderings of a Pilgrim in Search of the Picturesque*, this study demonstrates travel writing as a weapon of epistemic reclamation. Parkes and Begum inscribe themselves into histories and literatures that have long erased women's voices. They chart alternative cartographies—maps of emotion, rebellion, and cultural critique—that rupture hegemonic narratives and carve out fresh terrain for gendered mobility. Their journeys are not mere treks across land; they are symbolic revolts against the social prisons assigned to them.

Ultimately, this book asserts that women's travel writing in colonial contexts transcends the fetishization of the exotic. It stands as a political and creative insurgency, through which women have interrogated and dismantled the structures that sought to mute them. Whether through Parkes's romantic ambivalence or Begum's reformist precision, these texts roar a singular truth: when women seize the page, they wield the power to question, to reforge, and to reconfigure the world.

By centring two women who crossed not only continents but the entrenched fault lines of empire, gender, and ideology, this study reclaims the travelogue as a genre of insurgent intellect and transformative agency. Narrative motion becomes embodied defiance: every description a declaration of authority, every reflection an act of self-inscription. Fanny Parkes and Nawab Sikander Begum—though worlds apart—both hurled their voices into the empire's clamour, proving that true power lies in the stories we dare to tell. Their travelogues endure not simply as historical artifacts but as blueprints for renegotiating power, identity, and authorship in a world still haunted by the violent question of who is allowed to speak, and who is forced into silence.

Dr. Gurudev Meher
Associate Professor
Department of English
Ravenshaw University, Cuttack

Introduction

Travel writing is as old as movement itself. From the earliest human migrations to modern-day jet-set adventures, people have long felt compelled to document their journeys; not only to remember where they've been, but to understand who they are. A travelogue is never just about the route taken; it is a story of encounters, of curiosities stirred and fears confronted, of the self in dialogue with the world. It is history, geography, autobiography, and sometimes fiction, all stitched together in the traveller's voice.

But where did this urge to write about travel begin? Who were the first travel writers? And how has the form transformed across centuries and civilisations? This chapter offers a panoramic journey through the history of travel writing, from ancient records and religious pilgrimages to colonial explorations and feminist wanderings. It will highlight key figures, significant shifts in purpose and style, and the complex politics of who gets to travel and who gets to write about it.

The Origins: Travel as Record and Ritual

Long before printed books, there were oral stories. Some of the earliest travel "writings" were passed down by word-of-mouth tales of sea voyages, mountain crossings, desert pilgrimages, and encounters with the unfamiliar. Travel stories were crucial for ancient communities to share knowledge about trade routes, weather patterns, safe harbours, and friendly (or hostile) territories. But they were also full of wonder: monsters at sea, enchanted lands, and godly visions, making them as much myth as map.

In ancient Mesopotamia, *The Epic of Gilgamesh* (c. 2100 BCE) contains one of the first recorded journeys; a king seeking immortality in a world both spiritual and physical. In India, the great epics *Ramayana* and *Mahabharata* are deeply embedded with narratives of travel, exile, and return. Similarly, the Greek epic *The Odyssey* (8th century BCE) by Homer, with Odysseus' ten-year voyage home, can be read as one of the earliest and most influential travel tales in Western literature. These early stories often blurred the line between real and imagined, geographical and symbolic.

By the Classical period, travel writing began to take a more empirical form. Herodotus (5th century BCE), known as the 'Father of History,' included rich accounts of his travels across Egypt, Persia, and beyond, mixing observation with hearsay and reflection. His *Histories* are not travelogues in the modern sense, but they demonstrate how deeply travel was tied to knowledge production. The Romans followed suit—Strabo's *Geographica* (1st century CE) compiled detailed descriptions of the known world, while Pliny the Elder's *Natural History* offered a sprawling encyclopaedia of travel-based observations on flora, fauna, and cultures.

Meanwhile, travel was also intimately tied to religion. Pilgrimages to sacred sites were common across cultures, and many pilgrim-travellers recorded their journeys. In China, the Buddhist monk Faxian (c. 337–422 CE) travelled to India and wrote *A Record of Buddhist Kingdoms*, documenting his observations of Indian culture and religious practices. Centuries later, Xuanzang (602–664 CE) undertook a similar journey, writing his *Great Tang Records on the Western Regions*; both religious and ethnographic in tone.

Medieval Journeys: Faith, Trade, and the Unknown

In medieval Europe and the Islamic world, travel writing took on new shapes—part sacred duty, part geographical discovery, part narrative art. The most famous medieval travel writer, Marco Polo, left Venice in 1271 and spent over two decades journeying through Central Asia and China. His account, *The Travels of Marco Polo*, written down by a fellow prisoner after his return, sparked European imaginations and left a lasting impact on cartographers and explorers alike.

Simultaneously, in the Islamic world, travel writing was flourishing. Perhaps the greatest Muslim traveller of all time, Ibn Battuta (1304–1369), journeyed across North Africa, the Middle East, India, and even China. His narrative, *The Rihla*, or 'The Journey,' was as much a spiritual and scholarly account as it was geographical. Unlike Polo, who was seen as a curious outsider, Ibn Battuta often moved within the Islamic world, giving his writing a unique blend of familiarity and foreignness.

The medieval period also saw an increase in pilgrimage narratives, particularly among Christians visiting the Holy Land. These were often moralistic in tone, intended to inspire piety among readers. Yet, they also included descriptions of landscapes, cultures, and political tensions. Margery Kempe, a mystic from 14th-century

England, wrote what is considered the first autobiography in English, recounting her pilgrimage to Jerusalem with deeply personal reflections—a proto-feminist voice centuries ahead of her time.

The Age of Discovery: Conquest and Curiosity

The 15th to 17th centuries, often referred to as the Age of Exploration or Discovery, marked a turning point in travel writing. With the European voyages of Columbus, Vasco da Gama, Magellan, and others, travel narratives became instruments of empire. These were not just stories of personal adventure—they were reports for monarchs and financiers, justifications for colonization, and blueprints for conquest.

Christopher Columbus's letters and journals (1492 onward) narrate his encounters with the 'New World' in terms of wonder, wealth, and domination. The writings of Hernán Cortés and Bernal Díaz del Castillo recount the brutal conquest of the Aztec Empire, while glorifying their own roles. In these narratives, travel writing became entangled with imperialism, often exoticizing or demonizing indigenous peoples.

Yet, this period also witnessed more reflective, if no less biased, travel writers. Sir John Mandeville's fantastical *Travels* (14th century) blended myth with observation and was widely read well into the Renaissance. Later, the writings of Jesuit missionaries, like Matteo Ricci in China, were attempts at cultural diplomacy, attempting to bridge worlds even while representing them through a European lens.

This era also gave rise to the idea of the *Grand Tour*; a form of elite European travel undertaken by young aristocrats, particularly from Britain, in the 17th and 18th centuries. Visiting France, Italy, and Greece, these travellers kept detailed journals and letters, many of which were later published. The Grand Tour was about refinement, art appreciation, and political education, reinforcing class and cultural superiority.

Enlightenment and Empire: Science, Exploration, and the Exotic

In the 18th and 19th centuries, travel writing became a crucial part of the Enlightenment project. The world was to be measured, catalogued, and explained. Explorers were no longer just sailors or missionaries—they were botanists, linguists, cartographers, and colonial officers. James Cook's voyages to the Pacific were documented with meticulous precision, while the travelogues of Alexander von Humboldt helped shape early environmental sciences.

Travel writing at this time reflected a growing tension: the desire to objectively observe versus the impulse to judge and possess. Writers like Mungo Park in West Africa or Richard Burton in Arabia combined ethnographic detail with colonial gaze. The accounts of explorers in Australia, Africa, and India were not only scientific texts but also guides for imperial administration.

This period also saw the rise of female travel writers, though they were still exceptions in a male-dominated field. Figures like Lady Mary Wortley Montagu (who wrote extensively about Ottoman Turkey in the early 1700s) and Mary Kingsley (who travelled alone in West Africa in the 1890s) began to reshape the genre from within. Their writings were often deeply perceptive, self-aware, and politically engaged, challenging the assumptions of their male peers and readers.

The 20th Century: Modernity, Memory, and Movement

The 20th century brought dramatic changes to the way people travelled—and the way they wrote about it. With the rise of global transportation (trains, steamships, airplanes), travel became more accessible and widespread. Wars, migrations, and revolutions also created new forms of forced travel: exile, displacement, and diaspora became major themes in literature.

Travel writing during this era split in several directions. On one hand, popular travel memoirs and guidebooks flourished—Paul Theroux, Bruce Chatwin, and Pico Iyer continued the tradition of the literary traveller, combining observation with introspection. On the other hand, postcolonial writers began to radically question the authority of the travel narrator. Writers like V.S. Naipaul, Salman Rushdie, and Jamaica Kincaid wrote about travel not as a journey into the 'exotic,' but as a confrontation with empire, memory, and identity.

Simultaneously, feminist and queer travel writing gained momentum. Writers like Freya Stark, Rebecca West, and later Jan Morris wrote with a keen awareness of gendered space and marginalization, offering deeply personal and politically charged accounts of their travels. The travelogue was no longer a neutral form—it had become a platform for critique, storytelling, and radical imagination.

A Long Road: The History of Women's Travel Writing

Travel is as old as storytelling, and storytelling is as old as human memory. For centuries, tales of travel have stirred imaginations, bridged cultures, and redefined borders. Yet, when we leaf through the great travelogues of history, we find that women's voices often appear as whispers, footnotes, or shadows, if they appear at all. This absence is not due to a lack of movement or curiosity. Women have always travelled: as pilgrims and queens, as seekers and servants, as colonizers and colonized. What has changed, gradually and powerfully over time, is their ability to write about it, to record, reflect, and reframe the experience of mobility from their own perspectives.

This chapter traces the long, winding, and remarkable history of women's travel writing—from the cloisters of medieval Europe to the harem courts of the East, from the salons of Enlightenment Europe to the jungles of colonial Africa. In recovering this history, we find not just a genre, but a literary tradition that is bold, subversive, tender, and transformative.

Ancient Echoes and the Silences of Early History

When we speak of early travel writing, we often begin with Herodotus, Ibn Battuta, Marco Polo. But what of the women? In ancient literature, travel narratives by women are extremely rare—not because women did not move, but because they were rarely permitted to write or be published. What survives is often indirect: letters, oral histories, poems, or religious testimonies.

One of the earliest known female travel narratives comes from Egeria, a 4th-century Christian pilgrim from what is now Spain. Her *Itinerarium Egeriae*, written in Latin, documents her journey to the Holy Land. Her tone is observant, devotional, and deeply personal. She describes not just sacred sites but also the customs of local people, the challenges of the road, and her feelings of awe. In Egeria, we already see hallmarks of women's travel writing—attention to inner experience, cultural curiosity, and resilience in the face of difficulty.

Yet, for many centuries, such voices remained

anomalies. Travel was either inaccessible to most women or discouraged altogether. In patriarchal societies, a traveling woman was often seen as a transgressor—of gender roles, of safety, of propriety.

Medieval Journeys: Pilgrims and Mystics

In the medieval world, the most acceptable context for a woman's journey was religious pilgrimage. Women could move if they were seeking God—and even then, their movements were watched, questioned, or spiritualized.

Take Margery Kempe, a 14th-century mystic from England, whose *Book of Margery Kempe* (often considered the first autobiography in English) includes accounts of her pilgrimages to Jerusalem, Rome, and Santiago de Compostela. Kempe's writing is less about landscapes and more about spiritual transformation, divine visions, and public humiliation. Her voice is candid, emotional, and intense. Though dictated rather than penned by her own hand, the narrative is still hers—a woman asserting her right to journey both physically and spiritually.

These medieval accounts remind us that early women travellers were often constrained not just by geography but by expectations: they had to couch their narratives in religious legitimacy. Yet within these constraints, many found freedom. Travel allowed them to see the world, to meet others, to claim a voice—even if it had to be framed through piety or divine calling.

Renaissance and Early Modern Period: The Noblewoman Abroad

The Renaissance era, with its expanding horizons and courtly exchanges, allowed aristocratic women some room to move. Education and language learning were increasingly part of noble upbringing, and European women began to travel for diplomacy, marriage, and cultural enrichment.

Consider Lady Mary Wortley Montagu, an 18th-century English aristocrat whose *Turkish Embassy Letters* (published posthumously) remain a landmark in women's travel literature. Accompanying her husband, the British ambassador to the Ottoman Empire, she wrote vivid, witty, and intelligent letters describing life in Constantinople. Her observations of Ottoman women, especially those in harems, defied European stereotypes. She admired their freedom, fashion, and privacy, contrasting them sharply with English women's social restrictions.

Montagu's work is significant because it marks a shift. Here was a woman not only traveling but offering a counter-narrative to Orientalist fantasy. She was skeptical of imperial arrogance and invested in what we might now call 'cultural translation.' She was not merely observing the Other; she was questioning the Self.

Enlightenment and the Grand Tour: Exclusion and Emergence

The 18th century saw the rise of the 'Grand Tour' — a rite of passage for wealthy young European men, especially the British, to travel through continental Europe, absorbing art, politics, and culture. Women were often excluded from this tradition, though some carved out their own versions.

Elizabeth Craven, a playwright and novelist, undertook a journey through Europe and the Ottoman Empire and published *A Journey through the Crimea to Constantinople* (1789). Mary Wollstonecraft, the feminist philosopher, travelled through Scandinavia and published *Letters Written During a Short Residence in Sweden, Norway, and Denmark* (1796), which are as much philosophical meditations as they are travel narratives.

Wollstonecraft's letters are especially poignant—written in the wake of romantic betrayal, they reflect on solitude, nature, and national character. Her tone is introspective, ironic, and raw. Travel, for her, becomes a means of understanding not just the world, but the self. Her work laid the groundwork for the idea that women's travel writing can be both political and personal.

The 19th Century: Empire, Mobility and Literary Expansion

The 19th century was a golden age for travel writing—and for women's travel writing in particular. The expansion of empire, the rise of railways and steamships, and greater access to education meant more women could travel and publish.

But these opportunities were still shaped by empire. Many women travelled as part of colonial families, missionaries, or health seekers. Their narratives often reflect ambivalence: they are both part of imperial structures and subtly critical of them.

One of the most iconic women travellers of this time was Isabella Bird. Born in 1831 in England, Bird travelled extensively in Asia, the Americas, and the Middle East. Her *A Lady's Life in the Rocky Mountains* (1879) and *Unbeaten Tracks in Japan* (1880) are rich in detail, humour, and insight. Bird defied gender norms: she rode horseback through snow-covered passes, slept in tents, and wrote with a mix of awe and authority. She was not just writing for other women—she was writing as an equal to male adventurers.

Meanwhile, Fanny Parkes, a British woman living in India, wrote *Wanderings of a Pilgrim in Search of the*

Picturesque (1850), a travelogue that, despite its colonial framing, expresses deep affection for Indian culture. Parkes' curiosity, linguistic skills, and immersion in local life challenge the stereotype of the detached memsahib. Her work is vital in understanding how women engaged with the empire from within: "I found the native women to be more dignified and composed than I had ever imagined" (*Wanderings* 58).

In colonized regions, elite women also began to publish travel accounts. Nawab Sikander Begum of Bhopal, an Indian Muslim ruler, authored *A Princess's Pilgrimage* (1870), detailing her Hajj to Mecca. Her work combines religious devotion with a worldly awareness of political and social reform. Her ability to publish in English reflects both her proximity to British power and her own assertion of narrative control: "The Hajj is not merely travel—it is the surrender of the self" (*Princess's Pilgrimage* 29).

These examples show that 19th-century women's travel writing is not one thing. It is multivocal, global, and often paradoxical—a genre where class, race, religion, and language intersect in complex ways.

Early 20th Century: War, Modernity and the Quest for Meaning

The early 20th century brought with it new wars, new technologies, and new ways of seeing the world. Women's travel writing in this period became even more diverse in theme and tone.

Some, like Freya Stark, travelled into conflict zones. Stark's journeys in the Middle East—chronicled in books like *The Valleys of the Assassins* (1934)—were pioneering. She was fluent in Arabic, deeply knowledgeable about local cultures, and critical of British imperial policy. Her writing blends elegance with ethnography, memoir with adventure.

Others used travel writing to grapple with modern disillusionment. Rebecca West's *Black Lamb and Grey Falcon* (1941), written after her travels through Yugoslavia, is both a political treatise and a spiritual inquiry. West's prose is sharp, philosophical, and layered with historical reflection. The journey becomes a lens through which to understand the crisis of Europe between the wars.

In the colonies, indigenous and hybrid women voices began to appear—albeit slowly. Women in colonized countries began to claim authorship, though their works were often mediated, translated, or edited through colonial channels. Nevertheless, these early stirrings laid the foundation for a more global and decolonized travel literature in the decades to come.

Postcolonial and Contemporary Voices: Redrawing the Map

In the second half of the 20th century and into the 21st, the landscape of women's travel writing has radically expanded. The collapse of empire, the rise of feminism, and the globalization of publishing have enabled a chorus of new voices.

Women from formerly colonized nations began to tell their own travel stories—on their own terms. Writers like Aminatta Forna, Fatima Mernissi, Anita Desai, and Chimamanda Ngozi Adichie use travel across countries, languages, and identities—as a metaphor for survival, hybridity, and memory. Travel is no longer just physical movement; it becomes a vehicle for reimagining self and society.

Travel writing has also blended with memoir,

reportage, and fiction. Books like Elizabeth Gilbert's *Eat, Pray, Love* (2006) or Pico Iyer's works, though often controversial in tone, reflect a shift toward interiority and reflection, rather than conquest or description.

Crucially, digital technologies have further democratized the genre. Today, women blog, tweet, and vlog their journeys. Travel writing is no longer the exclusive domain of the published elite—it is a living, breathing archive of human movement.

Why Women's Travel Writing Matters

Women's travel writing is more than a literary genre—it is a mirror of changing freedoms, shifting frontiers, and evolving identities. It reveals not just how women saw the world, but how they saw themselves in relation to it. These narratives complicate the grand arc of history by inserting the personal, the embodied, and the emotionally intelligent into tales of geography and power.

To trace the history of women's travel writing is to follow a map of resilience and imagination. It is to listen to voices long muted, to read between the lines of empire, and to recognize that movement is, and always has been, a human right—not just a male one.

As we turn to the works of Fanny Parkes and Nawab Sikander Begum in this book, we do so not in isolation but in conversation with this long tradition. They are not anomalies. They are inheritors and innovators, part of a legacy that stretches across centuries, continents, and cultures—a legacy that continues, with every step and every story.

To travel is to venture into spaces unknown; to write about it is to assert presence, perception, and power. In the realm of literature, travel writing has long served as a medium through which experiences are translated, territories mapped, and identities constructed. However, for much of its history, the genre has been dominated by male voices—colonial officers, adventurers, and naturalists—whose gaze often reflected imperial ideologies and masculine worldviews. Against this backdrop, women's travelogues emerge not merely as alternative narratives but as radical acts of authorship and autonomy. This study examines two such remarkable works from the 19th century: *A Princess's Pilgrimage* by Nawab Sikander Begum of Bhopal and *Wanderings of a Pilgrim in Search of the Picturesque* by Fanny Parkes. These texts, composed in distinct cultural and historical contexts, converge in their assertion of female agency and the reimagining of travel as a space for self-articulation and cultural commentary.

Reclaiming the Map: Women's Travel Writing in the 19th Century

The 19th century marked a period of immense global flux: imperial expansion, industrial transformation, and epistemic shifts redefined the contours of both geography and identity. Travel became increasingly accessible to certain classes and genders, yet it remained a domain tightly regulated by social norms and imperial ambitions. For women, particularly, travel outside of domestic spheres was both a literal and symbolic breach of societal expectations. Writing about travel compounded this breach, it translated mobility into visibility, positioning women as narrators of their own journeys in a world where their voices were often mediated by others.

Women's travelogues in the colonial context frequently straddled the personal and the political, the spiritual and the secular. Unlike their male counterparts, who were often in the service of empire, women travellers wrote from the interstices simultaneously within and outside the structures of power. Their texts were shaped by and in turn shaped discourses of femininity, race, nationhood, and modernity. These narratives resist easy categorization; they oscillate between curiosity and critique, admiration and ambivalence, participation and protest. The genre, when appropriated by women, becomes a site of layered storytelling where subjectivity is foregrounded and experience is neither monolithic nor neutral.

Introducing the Texts and Their Authors

Nawab Sikander Begum's *A Princess's Pilgrimage*, first published in English in 1870, recounts her journey to the holy cities of Mecca and Medina. As the ruler of Bhopal, a princely state in colonial India, Sikander Begum occupied a rarefied position. She was both a sovereign and a subject independent in many administrative affairs, yet operating under the aegis of the British Raj. Her pilgrimage, undertaken in 1863–64, was not merely a spiritual quest but also a statement of political and personal autonomy. Her decision to travel, and more importantly, to publish her account in English (translated and edited by her British confidant Mrs. Willoughby-Osborne), reflects a complex negotiation of identity, faith, and imperial discourse.

In contrast, Fanny Parkes, the wife of a British civil servant, resided in India from 1822 to 1845. Her travelogue, *Wanderings of a Pilgrim in Search of the Picturesque* (published in 1850), documents her experiences across the subcontinent. Parkes was not a typical memsahib, her writings brim with fascination, empathy, and an eagerness to immerse herself in Indian customs, languages, and landscapes. While her position as a colonial subject complicates her sympathies, she repeatedly subverts the expected detachment of the colonial observer. Her text is a mosaic of sketches, anecdotes, recipes, reflections, and critiques, revealing a woman deeply engaged with the world around her, yet shaped inevitably by her own positionalities.

Though separated by nationality, religion, and purpose, both Sikander Begum and Parkes articulate a distinctly female experience of travel, one that is reflective, embodied, and often transgressive. This study reads their works not as isolated artefacts, but as dialogic texts that converse with each other and with the larger currents of gendered mobility and colonial modernity.

Methodology and Theoretical Framework

This study is rooted in an interdisciplinary approach, drawing from feminist literary criticism, postcolonial theory, travel studies, and life writing scholarship. It situates *A Princess's Pilgrimage* and *Wanderings of a Pilgrim* within both the canon of travel literature and the socio-political contexts of 19th-century colonial India. At the heart of this inquiry lies a set of questions: What does it mean for a woman to write about travel in a world governed by imperial and patriarchal structures? How do Sikander Begum and Parkes navigate their multiple identities religious, racial, cultural through the act of travel and its narration? To what extent do their texts resist or reinforce colonial ideologies? And how can these writings be read as semi-autobiographical explorations of selfhood?

This work employs a comparative framework that foregrounds both convergence and divergence. While recognizing the inherent asymmetries; one writer being a native ruler and the other a colonial expatriate and explore how both authors negotiate the binaries of insider/outsider, observer/participant, and subject/object. The analysis is organized thematically across subsequent chapters, examining motifs such as spatial agency, religious and cultural engagement, textual authority, and the politics of translation and voice.

Women, Space, and the Politics of Mobility

One of the central concerns of women's travel writing is the question of space—how it is accessed, inhabited, and described. For women like Sikander Begum, traversing public spaces was a radical act, especially when religious pilgrimages were largely the domain of male piety. Her travel defies the expected seclusion of noble Muslim women and asserts a right to visibility in both physical and textual domains. In writing about Mecca and Medina, she claims interpretive authority over spaces deeply coded by gender, faith, and colonial surveillance.

Similarly, Fanny Parkes' wanderings across India challenge the spatial restrictions often imposed on European women in the colonies. Her willingness to travel independently, to engage with Indian women and enter their zenanas, subverts the usual narrative of the secluded memsahib. Her descriptions are animated by a tactile curiosity about fabrics, rituals, landscapes, that lends her text an almost ethnographic texture. Yet this immersion is never entirely free of imperial privilege; it is precisely her colonial position that enables such access and mobility, even as she critiques certain aspects of British rule.

Thus, both authors deploy travel not just as physical movement, but as a strategy of spatial and epistemological reclamation. They write themselves into maps from which they might otherwise be erased, and in doing so, they challenge dominant cartographies of gender and empire.

Writing the Self: Autobiography and Authority

Another important dimension of these texts is their semi-autobiographical character. While not conventional autobiographies, both *A Princess's Pilgrimage* and *Wanderings of a Pilgrim* are deeply self-revealing. The narrators do not merely describe what they see; they offer meditations on their roles as women, as subjects of political and spiritual systems, and as authors who must justify and shape their authority.

Sikander Begum, writing under the constraints of royal decorum and colonial expectation, constructs a voice that is simultaneously devout and diplomatic. Her reflections are peppered with insights into governance, reform, and the condition of women, revealing a ruler who is also deeply aware of her symbolic import. The presence of a British translator/editor further complicates her voice, raising questions about authenticity, agency, and textual mediation.

Parkes, on the other hand, enjoys a greater degree of authorial freedom, but she too must navigate the conventions of her time. Her narrative persona oscillates between the enthusiastic amateur and the quasi-anthropologist, between the affectionate guest and the critical commentator. Her use of the picturesque trope, common in colonial travel writing is both strategic and ironic, allowing her to play with aesthetic conventions while embedding subtle critiques of imperial ideology.

In both cases, writing becomes a site where identity is not merely recorded but actively produced. These women are not just travellers; they are narrators, interpreters, and historians of their own lives.

The Colonial Gaze and Its Discontents

Inevitably, the texts examined here are shaped

by the pervasive gaze of empire. Whether it is Parkes' romanticization of Indian rituals or Sikander Begum's need to perform loyalty to the British crown, both writers engage with colonial power in ways that are complex and often contradictory. Yet, it is precisely in these contradictions that resistance can be found.

Sikander Begum's narrative may seem deferential at times, but it also subtly asserts sovereignty, over space, over narrative, and over interpretation. Her attention to social reform, her critiques of certain customs, and her decision to publish in English all signal a modernizing impulse that resists simplistic categorization as either traditionalist or imperial puppet.

Parkes, too, defies easy labelling. Her admiration for Indian art and culture coexists with moments of orientalist essentialism. But she consistently foregrounds her emotional and intellectual responses, privileging experience over doctrine. Her writing complicates the notion of the memsahib as aloof and prejudiced, offering instead a portrait of a woman deeply engaged, if not always critically aware.

By placing these two texts in conversation, this study seeks to uncover the ways in which colonial binaries are both enacted and unsettled in women's travelogues. It argues that even within constrained circumstances, women travellers found ways to write back: sometimes subtly, sometimes boldly, against dominant narratives.

Travelogue is a film, book or illustrated lecture about the places visited by or experiences of a traveller. It is the amalgamation of two words travel and monologue which combines to form travelogue. The main purpose of a travelogue is connecting travel with building social relationships. The more you travel, the more people you meet and the more you communicate, which helps you build social relationships. Travel writing celebrates the differences in manners and customs around the world.

The essence of adventure lies in taking risks and exploring the unknown, so it is hardly surprising to find that early travel accounts tended for the most part to be written by men, who moved more freely in the public sphere. The great sagas of knightly questing (such as *the North Sagas* and the Arthurian *cycle*). Also, seafaring exploration (such as *The Odyssey* and *The Lucidas*) are also male narratives with women as the objects of desire or destination points rather than active co-travellers, though the figure of the warrior princess roaming the world in the search of adventure was popular in renaissance epics like *Orlando furioso* and *Gerusalemme liberata*.

During the sixteenth and seventeenth centuries when men journeyed in search of fortune and experiencing the new worlds that were opening up beyond the frontiers of Europe was explicitly gendered, since the idea of man as heroic risk-taking traveller underpinned not only the great travel narratives of the next centuries, but much of the travel writing of the twentieth century also.

Alongside the myths of the heroic explorer, are other kinds of narratives, some of which have been produced by women. The travel text as ethnography, or social commentary transcends gender boundaries and increasingly in twentieth century male and female travellers have written self-reflexive texts that defy easy categorisation as autobiography, memoir or travel account. There is also in British travel writing, a tendency of self-deprecation and irony, a style of writing that has both Henry Fielding and Jane Austen as its antecedents, despite the fact that did not move beyond the confines of southern England.

In the circumstances of the paucity of the female voice and its representation in the seventeenth century sources of subcontinent, Europe travel narratives present several cases of women in their everyday life and activities in diverse frames. Women were generally in the corners of the sphere but through travelogues women started to come to the center rather than staying in the periphery.

Previously many of the early female travel writers were often nuns, aristocrats or diplomats' wives that gave their husbands company on foreign missions. By the nineteenth century, it became more common to find women with their own fortunes; these pioneers were intent on seeking strange lands and exotic countries without accompaniment and writing about their discoveries or publishing journals along the way.

Why women began to travel is the main question. Women began to travel for many personal and political reasons. Some women sought to further a cause, like missionary work, while others travelled to satisfy personal curiosities of 'exotic' lands. Most women, however travelled to escape gender oppression in Europe. One form of gender oppression had manifested in scholarly and scientific writing, in which women scholars were not taken seriously. This was especially clear in attitudes towards women who researched and collected data. So, women travelled to create a space for their research. In India, this proved to be a successful method of advancement in anthropology.

White women were admitted into harems and *zenanas*, the homes of hundreds of eastern women for the purpose of study. Men, however, were not allowed into these female dwellings. This allowed women that had come abroad to study and have expertise in an area where men had no access (Ghose 10). Race provided women with immediate empowerment (Ghose 9). White women travellers were hailed for their advancement of feminism. Many of the women were surprised at this honour for their intent was not political. Yet whether women travelled for a political purpose or not the power they gained in foreign lands as opposed to at home caused them to re-examine their position (Blunt 124).

Many of the observations made by women travelling to east concerned the indigenous people (Stevenson 10). Women viewed the people of the 'orient' from many different personal positions. Some female travellers identified with people of the land as objects of study. This relation of marginalization allowed feminist travellers to advance the status of European women by showing gender hierarchy in another context. Women's travel writing, long considered the genre of novelists-manqués and second-rate writers, is a rich source for teaching world history. Recent scholarship has swept away old prejudices, and a substantial secondary literature exists on different aspects of this genre, in itself an indication of its growing importance. What, then, are its advantages as a source for teaching world history? In the first place, the body of literature is vast, spread over time and space. As early as the 15th century, women were recording impressions of their travels (*The Book of Margery Kempe*, 1436). Since then, not only have hundreds of women of all nationalities put pen to paper to describe their travels, but they have done so while trekking to every corner of the world.

Second, the background of these writers is varied — from the aristocratic Lady Mary Wortley Montagu, who accompanied her husband to Turkey when he took up his ambassadorial post in 1716, to the intrepid Alexander David-Neel, who honed her traveling skills by repeatedly running away from home as a child and went on to become the first Western woman to enter Lhasa, the forbidden city of Tibet.

Housewives, missionaries, settlers, professionals, and sensation seekers have all contributed to existing travelogues so that motivation, social background, gender expectations, and the reception of women's writing are among the many issues that can be introduced into discussions of the topic. Third, travel literature consists of the impressions of one culture viewing another, and women's travel literature of one gender viewing others. It is, therefore, an excellent way of introducing concepts of cultural difference and discussing the way in which gender does, or does not, shape perceptions. Finally, travelogues often tell us as much, if not more, about the culture of the author as that of the subject matter, thus making them doubly valuable as sources.

By studying the indigenous peoples, women were able to rise to the status of the white male in scholarly writing and in literature. These women behaved paternalistically towards the natives, as white men acted towards them. Female European researchers who objectified native women were very critical of the people and the land they saw around them. Marie Postans, an English traveller represents many of the superior attitudes of the Europeans. In the following example, she writes of Hindu holidays and their interference with daily life: "Hindu holidays interfere sadly with the labours of the working classes" (Ghose 35). Postans' words re-emphasize the idea that the Indian way of living is lazy and fun-loving thus being unsuitable for the development of their own people. Postans' documentation of

Indian behaviour supported an existing belief in the Puritan work ethic during the nineteenth century. By describing the Indian population as lazy, the European population, in contrast, became sober and hard working. According to colonial belief, it was only through better European schooling and exposure to English enlightenment that would lead to an advancement of the Indian people (35). Another example is illustrated within the context of the remarks made by white women about women's behaviour in the harem or zenana in India. Many conservative white women viewed Indian women in harems as over-sexed and demented. White women contrasted their own behaviour to the behaviour of Indian women. As Isabella Bird claims:

I have lived in Zenanas, and have seen the daily life of the secluded woman, and I can speak from bitter experience of what their lives are–the intellect dwarfed, so that a woman of twenty or thirty years of age is more like a child of eight, intellectually; while all the worst passions of human nature are stimulated and developed to a Fearful degree: jealousy, envy, murderous hate, intrigue, running to such an extent that in some countries I have hardly ever been to a woman's house without being asked for drugs with which to disfigure the favourite wife, or to take away the life of the favourite wife's infant son. (Ghose 63)

Bird's description of the native population makes Europeans seem superior in intelligence and morality. She views the "child-like" Indian woman and believes that Indians need to be saved from their own downfall. As with many English, Bird felt that Indian people left alone without the enlightenment of the Europeans were doomed to destroy themselves.

Bird and Postans were two of the many imperialist women who contributed to the discourses of Orientalism. Their personal opinions of natives represent the attitudes of the majority of Victorian women who wrote and studied the women of the East and Africa. Below are quotes from various women whose travel journals also helped to shape Victorian attitudes towards the non-Western peoples.

Travel is sacred. Travel is a quest. Travel is an escape. Travel is a passion! It is enlightening, a distraction, a novelty, a dream fulfilled. It may inspire joy, terror, longing - often, all three. Women explorers and travellers are a special breed. Some were also great writers, recording their cross-cultural impressions with stunning vividness, blending history, myth, technology, and poetic imagination.

A dozen other women who boldly crossed international barriers often to encounter the most patriarchal cultures of their time are focused on in this delightful book - a significant contribution to travel literature as well as to women's studies. For me, travel writing is something very unrestrictive since it can be indulged in many genres. It includes everything from armchair travel writing to journaling while on an expedition to war correspondence to writing about poverty.

Throughout the ages, women have travelled and written about their experiences. Whether for pleasure, pilgrimage, or work, the stories of these women travel writers are an inspiration for modern women who venture off the beaten track.

Travel writing by women is more than about places - it's about how women cope with being women in a foreign land. It took the 18th century to see a dramatic proliferation of travel writing by women - again, largely because more women were learning to write.

Travel was also becoming more common, for leisure as well as business. Women often accompanied their husbands on trips and had plenty of free time to write their memoirs and tales of travel. People were also beginning to travel longer distances - especially the English, who wandered not only to the sunny South of Europe but far afield to Africa and Asia. A wave of intrepid English women travellers left their mark on literature during this period. Elizabeth Craven wrote about her travels through Crimea and Constantinople - and her description of the Ottomans was scathing: they were clumsy, lazy, politically corrupt, and corpulent - and Turkish coffee was bad. The editorial (as opposed to descriptive) style of writing was being shaped but often, the comparisons fared badly, with new lands comparing poorly to back home.

Dame Stark was one of the first Western women to travel through the Arabian deserts. She often travelled alone into areas where few Europeans - and even fewer women - had ever been.

French woman Alexendra David Neel made history in the early 1900s by walking, disguised as a male beggar, from China across Tibet and into the Forbidden City, whisch she was the first Western woman ever to enter. She lived more than a century - and surprised her local authorities by requesting a new passport at the ripe old age of 100.

The publication of travel narratives allowed English readers to learn about and to experience the world without leaving their homes. From the grand tour to more specific, information-gathering missions writing and publishing narratives of their observations and experiences for readers back home. However, while first hand through travel was culturally understood to be the best means of acquiring knowledge that very few could afford to do. Travel writers, usually upper-class white males would gather information about foreign lands and relay it to waiting readers in their houses.

Mary Louise Pratt explains that travelogue helped to construct "the rest of the world" for readers, while also impacting knowledge in important areas such as sciences. Certainly male travel authors dominated the market on published travel narratives. Fewer than twenty travel narratives were written by women during the colonial period. Since, travellers were generally male and of a higher social class, the construction of the outside world was created through a specific masculine Gaze one that grew increasingly imperialistic over the course of the colonial era.

Thus, it is vital to study the narratives that were written by female travel writers during the colonial era which provided the readers with another perspective with which one would view the world. It provides the way in which travel narratives are examined within the context of eighteenth century cultural, literary and political discourses. Women travel writers who wished to publish their narratives faced the daunting experience of being judged on a moral level by the reading public. According to Kristi Siegel, women travel authors had to form some 'narrative credibility' while also countering attacks against their feminity prompted by their so called un-natural and inappropriate behaviour of writing about their travels. Because these female travellers were stepping out from the domestic space of the home to the public sphere of travelling and publishing, they needed to construct an ethos for themselves that showed how they could be both feminine and a writer traveller.

Moreover, as Siegel states, there is a prevalent

"rhetoric of peril" that surrounds women travellers; a large part of the fear of women travelling has as much to do with fears about morality (such as what 'worldly' customs they might learn or what they might be tempted to do once outside of the 'civilised' world) as it does with safety. James Fordyce, in his sermons to young women (1766) cautions women against letting an education, which female writers needed in order to write, lead them to 'display' themselves in public or aspire "to shine anywhere but in their proper sphere (Dolan 43). For eighteenth century public women's bodies being out in the world seemed to be the most objectionable part of travel writing because a woman's place was in the domestic sphere. Women travellers constructed their experiences of travelling as ways of knowing and learning about the world, aligning them with larger cultural and epistemological discourses that privileged experience as a means of knowing. Experience, as the culturally constructed mode of knowing that underlies the truth value of a travelogue; sets travel narratives apart from other genres and is contingent upon physical accessibility. Issues of class clearly play into which women's experiences are available and how they construct their subjectivity within text. Female travellers were few, and those who did travel were invariably white, upper-class women with the means to do so. For example; based on their access to royalty and the manner in which they spoke of different social classes while abroad, it is clear that Montagu and Craven enjoyed much different experiences than Falconbridge and Wollstonecraft, both of whom were middle-class. Moreover, travelling put women physically into the public sphere in a way that other writing and publishing did not.

    Writing other genres such as the poetry or the novel,

could take place from the comfort of the domestic sphere. However, because travel writing demanded embodiment and exposure in the public sphere, women travel writers were more corporeally vulnerable than writers in other genres.

However, as more women's narratives about their travels were published, they began to challenge about what Vivian Jones refers to as 'the gendered control knowledge'.

The two books chosen for my research are also women travelogues. The first book is going to deal with is *A Princess's Pilgrimage* Nawab Sikander Begum's "A pilgrimage to Mecca". It was translated from Urdu to English by E.L. Willoughby Osborne. It shows how a woman can write travelogues during the colonial period. She was the ruler of Bhopal, a Mahomedan Princess from colonised India and most importantly she was the 'other' woman. During that period women were regarded as other because of the patriarchal society. For her to write a pilgrimage was fine. But writing it in a way to attract audience was something very appealing. Osborne listed four reasons why she translated and was interested in begum's pilgrimage:
1. It is because no 'work' by an 'eastern lady' had, to her knowledge, ever been   published
2. Very few European travellers had visited Mecca
3. The opportunity of viewing things from an oriental point of view is a novel one
4. Lastly because the author had already earned herself a reputation in India and   England   for the sagacity, shrewdness and enlightenment of her administration, as well as her loyalty toward British government during the 'Sepoy War'.

It shows the courage and grit of an Indian woman

from a minority community and still doing the things which a man cannot dare.

In analysing this narrative this research will highlight three main themes. First, it will examine the text's location within an Islamic tradition of travel writing as negotiated within a colonial context. Issues of motivation, audience, structure and style will be addressed, as well as the possible reasoning behind the book's published form. It will then seek to identify ways in which notions of the self were depicted in this narrative, questioning whether Sikander's main aim was to chart a personal journey of faith, as one may expect, or craft an identity more closely related to political concerns. In the third section, it will turn to investigating the Begum's perception of Arabia as the 'other' as an alternative construction of the 'orient'. Together, this analysis will provide an insight into a spiritual journey that while influenced by the colonial milieu, remained distinct from any European experience of travel. It is true that during colonial period it was hard to show your own view and Begum being from a minority community, writing a Muslim journey in a colonial environment was something of a new kind.

In her article on South Asian accounts of the *Hajj*, Barbara Metcalf has charted the emergence of this genre from the eighteenth century, suggesting that it is very much a 'modern phenomenon'. She makes this point on the basis that pre-modern South Asian Muslims were curiously silent about their experiences on hajj, even when they took the time to prepare their memoirs. Gulbadan, for instance, made no mention of her seven-year pilgrimage to the Hijaz in her narrative account of the reigns of her father, brother and nephew, the Mughal emperors Babur, Humayun and Akbar. It shows how women were from higher communities also were not in a position to write. However, Sikander broke the world to make people realise that anyone can write whether it be from a majority community or from minority community. The importance of the colonial context is also evident in that Sikander's published work that clearly directed at a British or at least British in India- audience.

The above-mentioned text also drew a number of parallels in describing what the ruling Begum observed in Arabia with European practices, thus making it intelligible for british readership as well. Yet another sign of the intended British audience were the illustrations, which included 'views' of Bhopal as well as a photograph of the author herself. This latter feature in particular is very rare in south Asian accounts of *hajj* most likely on account of the suspicion with which iconography tends to be viewed in Muslim cultures. Begum's reputation for loyalty, as established during the sepoy war was thus on show to be admired by British readers and the matter of dedication, not included until after Sikander's death and apparently at the initiative of Mrs Osborne, raises the question of the latter's influence over the final form and content of the published work. Sikander was having the courage to question the situations in mecca as well. She has beautifully described about the situations of the pilgrimage. She also described the administrative matters of Mecca. Sikander portrayed herself as every bit the reforming princess the improving landlord modelled in the estate- holders of Britain that imperial overlord expected her to be. Her critiques of Arabia's officials depicted in this narrative as corrupt and decadent as 'oriental despot' of the British imagination that demonstrates the degree to which she has internalised these ideals and become active in their reproduction. She had the power as well as mind to play and think how to construct perfect administration.

Also, she discussed about the Arabian women as noisy, large-made and they displayed great muscular strength than the men. She also expressed disapproval with their habit of singing which had not a slightest pleasure but is rather disgusted. Another feature of Arabian society that garnered the special attention of ruling Begum was their sanitary arrangement both in terms of their 'very dirty' houses and 'untidy' dress. This shows how seriously Sikander was taking her travel. And bringing the negative points of a place during the colonial period was not a simple thing because no one during the colonial habe ever tried to display the original view of the sacred place of Mecca.

The second book is Fanny Parkes' *Wanderings of a Pilgrim in Search of the Picturesque*. It deals with her experiences in India. The collection and Fanny Parkes' published recollections of her travels in India appear to have given her a public legitimacy and authority lacking before she went to sub-continent. India and her experiences there changed her and enabled her to construct a new identity for herself. Knowing India first-hand was a claim frequently made by travel writers of the period when attempting to add authority and authenticity to this aspect of imperial project. Fanny's sense of 'knowing' was enhanced by gathering objects from the sub-continent and by sharing her acquired knowledge with a public eager to see the curiosities, the monsters and the idols that she took with her when she left India forever. She was amazed by the beauty of India. She celebrated the facts.

Wanderings suggests that Fanny distinctly wished to be understood as someone who had formed knowledge and expertise through authentic experience. With little means of corroborating the events that Parkes described in *Wanderings it* is difficult to ascertain that exact nature of her experiences in in India and the gaps between those experiences and the stories she told about them. *Wanderings of a Pilgrim in search of the picturesque* analyses the way she sought to present herself to the public on her return to Britain. When she returned to the metropole this chapter argues her writings and collection lent her authority in an almost exclusively masculine society of Indian experts. She gained entry to a social world to which she might not otherwise have been admitted and formed a life independent of her own life. On returning to Britain then, she publicly utilized her collection to validate and enhance her experiences. In analysing these writings and practices of exhibition, this chapter seeks to show how a woman linked to the East India Company was able to use her experiences of the subcontinent to effect on her return. It also illustrates the way in which one Company woman took advantage of her colonial experiences to collect, describe and display Indian material culture. At the same time, it demonstrates how her collections, their display and description, generated perception of expertise which gave her legitimacy in the male dominated world of collecting, as well as status and independence in metropolitan society. Fanny learnt how to run a house with a multitude of servants, enjoyed riding her Arab horse on the maidan at dusk after the heat of the day, took lessons in Hindi and Sanskrit, and started to explore the intricacies of Indian culture. In particular, she also became 'very anxious to visit a zenana, and to witness the lives of the high-class Indian women kept in seclusion behind its closed doors. Fanny had 'collected an empire' for herself that liberated her from the constraints of life in the metropole and through the exotic objects she had acquired she gained an independence ' a life independent of her own life' that opened a new world for her. Her detailed and valuable knowledge of another culture and her understanding of its social world particularly that of the zenana, a world closed to men gave her status in a metropolitan, masculine society. Her collection, initially a jumble of the curiosities, the monsters etc. It now assumed an importance as a discrete entity, allowing those British men and women who saw it to visualise their empire. Fanny also shared her love for India with others through the journals and letters, which were published as the travelogue. They provided a space in which her experiences of India and the stories she wished to tell then could shape a broader conception of who she was and what she had achieved. Her access to the intimate world of the exclusively female zenana of high caste Indian women and her descriptions of this offered a rare insight into an exotic world and enhanced the picture of the colonized for a fascinated metropolitan public. She turned what she had gained in India: independence, knowledge, and experience into a new life for herself in metropole. Her expertise brought her status and legitimacy in this metropolitan world.

For male writers it was next to impossible to go into this world and search for the truth but it is only through a woman that can get a glimpse into the domestic front. Both the travelogues which I have taken for my research holds a very different notion in the colonial period. The travelogues stand out differently from the travelogues available to us then.

While comparing these two texts, lots of similarities and differences will be observed and analysed.

Women's travel writing, once dismissed as sentimental, anecdotal, or less serious than its male counterpart, has undergone a remarkable transformation in recent scholarship. It is now appreciated not just for its literary and historical value, but for the way it sheds light on the lives, thoughts, and inner worlds of women who dared to venture beyond the boundaries set for them by society, empire, and gender. This shift in recognition has allowed figures like Nawab Sikander Begum and Fanny Parkes to emerge not only as travellers and observers but as vital commentators on identity, power, and place in the 19th century.

Travel writing has long served as a mirror—reflecting not just the outer world, but the identity, values, and politics of the traveller. For women, especially during the colonial period, this mirror was more than reflective; it was transformative. Through their travel narratives, women were able to step beyond domestic boundaries, redefine themselves, and often challenge the power structures of their time. This literature review explores the scholarly conversations surrounding women's travelogues, with a special focus on the works of Nawab Sikander Begum and Fanny Parkes, two authors who used their journeys to assert their voices in remarkably different ways.

Sikander Begum: A Voice from Within the Colonized World

Sikander Begum's *A Princess's Pilgrimage* is often seen as groundbreaking, not only because it details a woman's pilgrimage to Mecca in the 19th century but because it was written by a Muslim ruler of Bhopal a doubly marginalised figure in colonial discourse. Scholars such as Siobhan Lambert-Hurley have explored how Sikander's account is layered with more than religious devotion. It becomes a subtle form of political commentary. Her descriptions of Meccan society and governance are not just observations they are critical reflections shaped by her experiences as both a Muslim and a monarch under British rule.

Rather than presenting herself as a passive traveller, Sikander emerges as a reformist thinker. She doesn't hesitate to critique the inefficiencies of Arabian society or point out where reform is needed. At the same time, she is navigating a delicate line: writing to a British-influenced audience while maintaining her Islamic identity. Scholars have pointed out that her travelogue helps to reframe the narrative around Muslim women, portraying them as thoughtful, opinionated, and capable of leadership—qualities rarely attributed to them in colonial literature.

Fanny Parkes: A British Gaze Complicated by Curiosity

In contrast, Fanny Parkes represents the colonial outsider yet one who took an unusually empathetic approach to the culture she was living in. Her *Wanderings of a Pilgrim in Search of the Picturesque* is filled with admiration, curiosity, and sometimes bewilderment about Indian life. Rather than distancing herself from the people around her, Parkes made efforts to learn local languages, understand customs, and explore spaces like the zenana, spaces that were completely off-limits to British men.

Scholars like Shampa Roy have explored Parkes' writing to show how she straddled a fine line between colonial observer and cultural participant. While her admiration for India is sincere, her travelogue still reflects the biases of her time. She sometimes falls into exotic descriptions or subtly reinforces British superiority, even when expressing appreciation. Still, her work remains important for offering a more layered perspective than many of her contemporaries. Her writings show a woman negotiating both gender and empire finding a space for her own voice within the complex framework of colonial rule.

Bringing the Two Together

When read side by side, the writings of Sikander Begum and Fanny Parkes offer a rich dialogue. They come from different worlds—one writing from within colonised India, the other from the colonising power—but both challenge the dominant narratives about women's roles and capabilities. Where Sikander uses her position to critique and reimagine Islamic and colonial authority, Parkes uses her curiosity to build unexpected bridges between cultures, even while entangled in imperial ideology.

Recent scholars of travel writing like Sara Mills, Mary Louise Pratt, and Indira Ghose have emphasized how women's travel narratives are often shaped by the expectations placed upon them. These women were not just writing about foreign lands, they were also navigating ideas of propriety, morality, and female decorum. Their texts reflect this tension. Yet this very struggle also makes their work powerful. It shows women claiming intellectual and political space through the act of travelling and writing.

Together, the works of Sikander Begum and Fanny Parkes reveal the importance of women's travel writing as more than personal diaries. These texts are rich cultural and political artefacts, helping us understand how women have shaped and reshaped their identities through movement, observation, and storytelling.

Nawab Sikander Begum: Power, Pilgrimage, and the Politics of Presence

Sikander Begum's *A Princess's Pilgrimage* stands as a powerful testament to what it meant for a woman, especially a Muslim ruler from colonized India to write about a journey that was spiritual, political, and personal. Her travel to Mecca in 1863 was not merely a religious obligation, but an act of self-assertion at a time when Muslim women were expected to remain invisible in the public sphere. Siobhan Lambert-Hurley, who has edited and written extensively about this text, highlights its remarkable layers. She argues that the book is not just a narrative of hajj; it is also a political document, shaped both by colonial expectations and by the author's own desire to assert her identity in a world that often-erased voices like hers.

What is particularly striking is the way Sikander's observations of Mecca go far beyond religious devotion. She critiques the administrative failures she sees, she comments on sanitation, on the behaviour of Arabian women, and on the decadence of the local elite. In doing so, she reflects both the ideals of Islamic reform and the influences of British political thought, positioning herself as a modern, enlightened ruler in the eyes of a British audience. Lambert-Hurley emphasizes that this dual positioning, being both a devout Muslim and a loyal ally of the British that makes her text a rich site of negotiation and identity construction.

Sikander Begum's narrative defies easy categorization. It is part travelogue, part political commentary, part self-fashioning. And it is precisely this hybridity that gives it power. In a colonial context where indigenous voices were often silenced or mediated through others, Sikander's authorship is both rare and radical.

Fanny Parkes: Curiosity, Collection, and Contradictions of Empire

Fanny Parkes, by contrast, comes from the other side of the colonial equation. A British woman living in India, her *Wanderings of a Pilgrim in Search of the Picturesque* is a detailed, vivid account of her years spent in the subcontinent. Parkes was not a passive resident; she was curious, energetic, and unusually open to learning about Indian life. She learned local languages, collected Indian art and artefacts, and sought out women's spaces like the zenana to understand how Indian women lived.

Scholars such as Shampa Roy have shown how Parkes used her position as a woman to access domains denied to her male counterparts. Her ability to enter and describe the zenana is not just a point of cultural curiosity, it becomes a source of power. In a world where male colonial officers wrote about Indian women based on second-hand accounts or stereotypes, Parkes brought first-hand experience. This gives her writing an authenticity and richness that remains significant today.

But her work is not without contradictions. Like many Europeans of her time, Parkes was shaped by colonial ideologies, and this sometimes comes through in her writing. While she often expressed deep affection for India and admiration for its people, she also perhaps unconsciously, reinforced certain colonial narratives. For example, her descriptions sometimes slide into exoticism or reflect an implicit sense of cultural superiority. Scholars have debated whether Parkes was subverting empire by embracing Indian culture, or whether she was ultimately complicit in reinforcing it.

Regardless of where one stands in that debate, what is clear is that Parkes' travelogue reflects a woman navigating the colonial world in her own way, sometimes resisting, sometimes conforming, but always observing and writing with a strong, distinct voice.

Comparative Insights: Two Women, Two Worlds, One Shared Struggle

When read together, the travel writings of Sikander

Begum and Fanny Parkes reveal fascinating similarities and striking contrasts. One was a Muslim ruler writing from inside the colonized world; the other, a British expatriate writing from within the colonizing structure. Yet both used the act of travel and the medium of writing to carve out space for themselves in a male-dominated world.

Both women wrote with great clarity and detail, not just about the external journey, the roads, the rituals, the landscapes but also about what these journeys meant to them as women. Their texts speak of identity: how it is constructed, challenged, and sometimes reinvented through the act of movement. They reveal the limitations women faced: whether imposed by religious tradition, colonial politics, or social norms but also how they found ways to stretch those boundaries, to claim knowledge, and to assert voice.

These travelogues also challenge the idea that women's writing is apolitical or confined to the domestic. On the contrary, both Sikander and Parkes address public issues i.e. religion, governance, gender roles, cultural practices with insight and intelligence. Their observations are sharp and often critical. They do not simply describe; they analyse, compare, and question.

In recent years, scholars have increasingly acknowledged how women's travel writing allows us to hear voices from the margins, voices that often tell a different story than the one recorded by imperial or male-authored narratives. Writers like Sara Mills, Mary Louise Pratt, and Indira Ghose have emphasized that women travellers often had to justify their presence in the public world, and their writings often reflect a tension between self-expression and social expectation. Yet this tension itself becomes productive, generating texts that are layered, complex, and deeply revealing. *Female Collecting and Curiosity in India and Britain* (Joanna Goldsworthy- 2018) outlines Fanny Parkes as a person, about who she is, why she is staying in India etc. It also deals with how her visit to India gave her curiosity to collect knowledge about India as well as Indian women. It also deals with the idea of Wanderings of a Pilgrim in search of picturesque, where it deals with her day-to-day affairs and her journals and long letters are also discussed. It also shows her emotional attachment with India while leaving the country; for instance:

And now the pilgrim resigns her staff and plucks the scallops hell from her hat- her wanderings are ended, she has quitted the East, perhaps for ever; surrounded by the curiosities, the monsters, that accompanied her from India the pleasure she derives from her sketches, and the sad sea waves, her constant companions, form for her a life independent of her own life". (Parkes 32)

The literature discussed above deals with the anxiousness and curiosity of Parkes while staying in India. *Women Travellers in Colonial India: The Power of Female Gaze* (Indira Ghose- 1998) draws on long neglected travel writings by British women in India. This study views different aspects that focuses on areas opposed to men, particularly in their encounters with Indian women in Zenana. Located at the cross-roads of feminist theory and colonial discourse theory, the article examines the power relations inscribed into the traveller's gaze. It justifies how travellers used their scope to do something good for the Indian women as well as women from the whole world. Its subtitle focuses on female gaze and female power. According to her, curiosity should be understood here as a sort of desire for adventure and for the difference associated with the other. Women travelogues during the colonial period had some social limitations with the availability of power as well. On one hand, Ghose details the particulars of women travellers' texts and draws attention to their plurality; on the other hand, she generalizes their split reactions to India. It acts as an expression of colonialisms own ambivalence as well as their contradictory inscription within both power and opposition. *Travel writing, history and colonialism: An analytical study* (Faraz Anjum- 2014) reflects on the major reasons for conceptualising Travel and Travel Writing where author traces the etymological origin of Travel and also writes about travel as a serious activity. According to the author travel is not only for our enjoyment it holds much stuff than that. He also defines travel writing as a multiple genre in itself which consists of other genres. According to him travel literature contributed to genres of the modern novel and the renaissance of autobiography. *The imperial sublime: English Travel writing and India* (Pramod K. Nayar- 2002) attempts to prove the point about the period of crisis for the English in India and how wars, corruption etc. led to Travel Writing. He discusses about the topography of Desolation and Improvement. He discusses about the search for socio-topographical refuge which can be taken as threatening act because of the absence of cultivation, people and refuge. A traveller loses its way and takes refuge in an indefinite land. The above literature reviewed suggests how travel literature emerged. *Ladies on the loose: contemporary female travel as 'Promiscuous' Excursion* (K.E. Cantreel-2011) explores how female travel narratives were read as excursions rather than expeditions, it was common for women authors to preface their travels with an apology. In many ways, the modern female traveller, like the early lady traveller is still a displaced woman. Women's solitary and unescorted travel, even in contemporary times is considered less common in the western world. With recurrent travel warnings constantly targeted at the female travellers. Previously those women who did travel openly into the world were often accused of flaunting the gendered norms of female decorum with their so-called unnatural and inappropriate behaviour. The continued harnessing taboo by popular media constitutes to shape contemporary patterns of female travels. Finally, it often emerges that even when female travel focuses specifically on an individual or collective female experience, it is still read in opposition to the long tradition of travelling men. In the light of such comments, there remains traceable difficulties for contemporary female travel writers. As travel is inherently gendered. It is from this site of trouble that new patterns of female travel will continue to emerge, distinguishably and defiantly, towards a much more colourful vista of general misrule. *Travel writing and gender* (Susan Basnett-2006) discusses how the essence of adventure lies in taking risks and exploring the unknown. It is hardly surprising to find that early travel accounts tended for the most part to be written by men. Men were allowed to move freely in the public sphere. The above literature available to us only shows how gender is biased in the context of travel also. From the old period to the modern period. *An Introduction to Travel Narrative* (Matti Hyvarein-2001) posits how Narrative is no doubt one of the great academic travellers of the last forty years. As such, there is nothing exceptional or sensational in this mobility: narrative simply belongs to the same group of travellers as 'culture', 'discourse', 'gender' and many others. Epistemic ruptures obviously encourage such fast transformations of the scholarly vocabulary. Many of these overlapping re-evaluations have been categorized under the more or less hyperbolic title of 'turn', be it linguistic, cultural, rhetorical, constructivist, or narrative. At least in the case of narrative, the term as such is highly ironic, as if there were one, distinct lineage of thought, and a clear turn of the storyline: a perfectly conventional story indeed. But by remembering to keep these terms descriptive rather than normative, and by presuming that all these turns are far from unitary one-plot stories, we may be entitled to reason that the turns pin down important aspects of a profound intellectual change, a change within a broader web of concepts. Perhaps more consideration should even be given to the possibility that narrative may not have travelled all alone, at least not all the way. With these reservations in mind, one can still contemplate the qualities and contexts that made narrative such a quick and agile traveller. *Gender and Travel Writing in India*(P. Chatterjee-

2012) explores how in Travel Narrative of the late 17th century, incidents involving gender relations appear regularly, sometimes the travel/ author narrates them in order to depict those relations, while in other to depict these relations, while in other instances, the tropes of gendered discourse need to be excavated from these representations in the travel narratives, this essays investigates the intricacies of the gender relations where identities are constantly formed and modified layers of meanings are created around descriptions of events, contradictions and conclusions are found in abandon and the bridges of understanding emerge and get dissolved frequently. In the circumstances of paucity of the female voice and its representation in the 17th century sources of the subcontinent, European travel narratives present several cases of women in their everyday life and activities in diverse frames. Although there is an abundance of mention of women, there are other problems with the travel narratives. The travel narratives seek to present men and women and their lives, but end up representing as much about the world view and communication networks of the travel/ author and fluid spaces in the area.

Ultimately, what the works of Sikander Begum and Fanny Parkes offer is not just a glimpse into two women's lives, but a window into a broader cultural and historical landscape, one in which women claimed the right to travel, to observe, to reflect, and above all, to write. Their legacies remind us that travel is never just about geography. It is about power, perception, and the journey toward selfhood.

Chapter I

The Search for Identity through Travelogues

"Identity is not found, the way Pharaoh's daughter found Moses in the bulrushes. Identity is built."

—Margaret Halsey

Identity crisis is a period of uncertainty and confusion in which a person's sense of Identity becomes insecure, typically due to a change in their expected aims or role in society. This chapter discusses some of the ideas that are implicit in this collection: the desire of travellers to discover that which is 'new'; the narrative negotiation between an outward self and an inner self; the concept that the writer's self is a fiction; the notion that writers use perceptual templates to understand and describe places; the transitional, liminal experience of passage; the dialogic nature of vision, which holds that the observer is also observed; and the constructed nature of place when it is construed as a story world.

In Colonial India, the social status of women seemed to be dependent on their men. The religious tradition ascribed for their humility and subordination to men in all matter. They were denied the opportunity of education and refinement. Except a few women of the upper classes, the life of general women was not worth living. In short, the access to social justice and equality were denied to them. They were unaware of their basic rights as individuals due to illiteracy, ignorance and economic subordinate through the age (Manu Smriti with six commentaries, 1886). Strange is the fact that when the Christian missionaries saw the deplorable condition of women in traditional Indian society. They were amazed and emotionally moved. The Christian missionaries aimed to spread their religion in India. Therefore, they opened school, asylums, dispensaries and orphanage to give relief to the poor and the needy Indian people. They succeeded in converting mostly the lower classes of Indian people. They failed to understand as to what they should do to save the women from burning alive. They desired to undertake from some 'Culturally Motivated' performance to end their crime. The first and foremost social problem that attracted enlightened opinion was the need for a better deal for women in society. In the abolition of the cruel rite of sati and infanticide, in the condemnation of child marriage and polygamy and popularization of widow remarriage in the abolition of *purdah* in provision of education facilities for women and economic opening to make them self-supporting and finally an equal share for women in the political life of the country by enfranchisement. This was the scenario during the colonial period of India, the 'self' was missing for the Indian women, which was led by some writers to change the above written.

Women travel writers found their own way to describe the same and get out of that situation. Travel also involves issues of identity. Sometimes, it even involves transformations of identity, as some of the extraordinary examples of many women travellers of the nineteenth century and early twentieth century appear to confirm. Isabella Bird, who journeyed through some of the most hostile regions of the world and recounts hardships that appear barely imaginable, was a semi-invalid who began her travels as a result of medical advice. Having cared for aged parents until the age of forty, she was diagnosed as suffering from a debilitating spinal complaint, acute insomnia and depression. These physical difficulties did not stop her from travelling to Hawaii, Japan, China etc. where she appeared to enjoy not only good health but also extreme fitness. The above example shows what travel can do for a woman.

Nawab Sikander Begum was a hereditary ruler of the princely state of Bhopal in colonial India. She travelled to *Mecca* with a retinue of a thousand people. On returning, she wrote a witty, acerbic account of her journey. In it, we could see the glimpse of a process by which notions of the 'self' could be redefined against a Muslim 'other' in the colonial environment. She was a ruler despite that she was searching for identity as Muslim. Also, she was standing for the whole oppressed women of India.

There were many instances which was discussed by Begum, one of that is the women of Arabia were, in particular, objects of her wrath on the basis that they were 'noisy', 'large-made' and displayed 'great muscular strength than the men' (Begum, 102). Some of this observation suggests that Arab women did not fulfil Sikander's expectations of modesty and demureness from the 'weaker sex' as they were rooted in Indian patriarchal values and coloured by Victorian notion of domesticity. She saw everything and somewhere wanted to change the current scenario of Indian women. She also took stand for minor Muslim community by writing herself for Indians as well as for the Britishers in India. This is her way of searching for self for herself as well as for other women.

Fanny Parkes was a traveller, collector and ethnographer. India and her experiences there changed her and enabled her to construct a new identity for herself. Wanderings suggests that Fanny distinctly wished to be understood as someone who had formed knowledge and expertise through 'authentic' experience. This illustrates the way in which one company woman took advantage of her colonial experiences to collect, describe and display Indian material culture. At the same time, it demonstrates how her collections, their display and description, generated a perception of 'expertise', which gave her legitimacy in the male-dominated world of collecting, as well as status and independence in metropolitan society. Having the courage to travel she discovers *Zenana* to witness the lives of the high-class Indian women kept in seclusion behind closed doors. She also fought with Indian patriarchal society to provide identity to the women. She also condemned the act of *Sati*. It shows her potentiality to deal with society and act according to the need. Identity plays a very crucial role in all genres. Travelogue is also known as a genre of quest. Quest of identity becomes the main theme in travelogue because when we travel, we counter variety of our individuality.

When we travel with a motive not that our identity changes it emerges with more refined identity. Women during the colonial period used this weapon to fire upon the patriarchal society. Parkes and Begum did the same thing they used their wanderings as a source of forming identity for themselves as well as for other women in India.

Travel, especially in the 19th century, represented more than physical movement; it symbolized transformation, liminality, and self-actualization. For women like Nawab Sikander Begum and Fanny Parkes, writing their journeys was an act of self-construction, a means to reclaim intellectual and existential autonomy. As theorist Mary Louise Pratt notes in her work on the 'contact zone,' travel writing is often a space where identities are formed and negotiated through cross-cultural encounters. For women in colonial contexts, the travelogue became not only a reflection of external geographies but also a deeply introspective map of the inner self—of longings, constraints, resistances, and assertions.

What is particularly notable in both *A Princess's Pilgrimage* and *Wanderings of a Pilgrim in Search of the Picturesque* is the way these women writers deploy travel as a metaphor for negotiating personal and political identity. Their journey is not just from one land to another, but from margin to centre—a movement toward epistemic authority in a world structured by male, colonial, and religious dominance:

The women, as I was the first European lady they had ever seen, examined my dress with the most minute attention. Some of the Begums and other ladies of distinction kissed my hands, and were all curious to hear my opinion of India. I praised their country, and told them I thought the Indian women very handsome. My interpreter, a respectable elderly woman, told them what I said; they seemed pleased and returned the compliment by saying, 'You are very beautiful, very beautiful indeed; but you are so white, you are not like a woman, you are like a spirit. (Parkes 215)

At last, the steward arrived and I told him that when the agent received a reply from Government, I would give up the House. The steward insisted that it must be vacated immediately, and as I would not accede to his request, he brought me a notice to quit. I replied that I would not quit until I received an answer from Government, but if the steward would bring back the sum of 300 rupees which I had paid him, I would go. He refused to return the money, and I in turn refused to vacate the house. The steward then left and brought with him several low fellows armed with sticks, and forcibly expelled me and my people from the house. (Begum 103)

Both Parkes and Begum are embedded within, and to varying extents, complicit in, the colonial matrix of power. Yet they also subvert it. Parkes, a British expatriate, reflects a dual consciousness: her writings display affection for Indian culture, yet sometimes slide into exoticism or latent superiority. Still, she offers nuanced descriptions of Indian domesticity, women's spaces, and rituals, claiming a kind of 'female ethnography' unavailable to her male peers. Through her engagement with the 'other,' she implicitly questions what it means to be a colonial woman in a land that she simultaneously admires and governs.

Sikander Begum, on the other hand, represents a rare voice from the colonized world—a Muslim ruler writing to a partially British audience. Her critiques of Meccan society, of Arabian women, and of inefficient religious administration are paradoxically both reformist and colonialized in tone. Her identity as a Muslim woman is not fixed but hybrid—inflected by Islamic reformist ideals, British modernity, and her own sovereign vision.

A crucial point of convergence in both texts lies in their semi-autobiographical nature. These are not traditional autobiographies, yet they reveal deeply personal dimensions: emotional turbulence, intellectual awakenings, moral judgments, and cultural reflections. As feminist theorist Sidonie Smith suggests, women's life writing often uses narrative as a 'space of agency' where personal memory intersects with historical discourse. Through self-representation, both Begum and Parkes construct an identity that is at once gendered, political, and mobile.

Sikander Begum, for instance, reflects on her own role as a ruler who must interpret Islamic traditions through the lens of administrative reform. Her writing demonstrates an internalization of colonial expectations—efficiency, hygiene, orderliness—while also advocating for Muslim solidarity and gender inclusion. In doing so, she reclaims the narrative space that had long excluded Muslim women.

Parkes, meanwhile, constructs herself as a woman who 'knows India'—an identity formed through tactile experience, linguistic immersion, and cultural empathy. Her travelogue is interspersed with domestic details, humorous anecdotes, and philosophical musings, all of which perform an identity that is intellectual yet emotionally textured. Her tone, while sometimes shaped by colonial confidence, is also self-aware and curious—a reminder that identity, especially in the travelogue, is never singular but always layered.

In both travelogues, the relationship between observer and observed is dialogic. As Bakhtin theorized, identity is often constructed in dialogue with the other; the gaze is never neutral. Begum's perception of Arabian society reflects not just a ruler's scrutiny but also a woman's confrontation with unfamiliar gender roles within Islamic cultures. Her critical descriptions—of 'muscular women,' unsanitary living conditions, and corrupt governance—serve a dual function: asserting her superiority as a modern Muslim monarch and reaffirming her identity as a reformist in an international Islamic community.

Parkes, meanwhile, turns her gaze upon Indian women with a complex mix of admiration, sympathy, and colonial fascination. Her vivid descriptions of zenanas, sari fabrics, puja rituals, and language learning are not just ethnographic; they are also self-reflective. Her ability to move between cultures allows her to write from a position that is both embedded and detached—a hallmark of what Homi Bhabha might call the 'third space' of cultural hybridity.

To write as a woman in the 19th century was to engage in resistance—not always radical, but often subversive. For Parkes, the act of documenting Indian life with affection was itself a quiet rebellion against the cold imperial gaze. For Begum, the decision to write in English, to critique Mecca, and to insert her voice into an Anglophone print culture dominated by male narratives, was a form of cultural defiance.

In both cases, travel becomes a vehicle for 'epistemic disobedience' (to borrow from Walter Mignolo). These women refuse to be silent spectators of empire or religion. Instead, they use the travelogue to stake a claim to intellectual territory. Identity, in this sense, is not just found—it is forged, word by word, against dominant discourses.

Access to space—both physical and textual—is central to identity formation. Sikander Begum's physical movement through sacred Islamic sites parallels her textual occupation of public discourse. As a veiled monarch travelling among men, and as a Muslim woman publishing in English, she breaks spatial and epistemological boundaries.

Parkes too traverses spaces deemed inappropriate for European women. Her physical mobility—riding horses, visiting villages, entering zenanas—is mirrored by her textual fluidity. She moves from the descriptive to the poetic, from the humorous to the didactic, creating a narrative that resists genre conventions and gender expectations.

In both cases, mobility is not just about changing places; it is about changing roles—about becoming subjects, rather than objects, of history.

In many ways, the travelogue becomes a kind of refuge—a space where women like Nawab Sikander Begum and Fanny Parkes can speak when history might otherwise have silenced them. For both women, writing wasn't just about chronicling a journey from one place to another; it was about reclaiming a voice, an identity, and a public presence. Through their words, they push back against the boundaries that were socially, politically, and even spiritually imposed on them.

Sikander Begum's voice is particularly compelling because of her context: a Muslim ruler from colonized India, stepping into the heart of the Islamic world and choosing to share her observations in English. It's a bold move, writing not only for her own people but also for the colonial audience watching from the sidelines. In doing so, she asserts herself as more than just a pilgrim. She becomes a commentator, a reformer, a woman of sharp intellect and strong will. Her identity, layered as it is, comes alive on the page, a part ruler, part believer, part critic of both East and West:

The ignorance of women is so profound, and their condition so degraded, that they are treated as mere chattels. Their seclusion, their want of education, and the continual din of superstition in their ears from childhood upwards, combine to render them helpless and slavish. (*A Princess's Pilgrimage* 45)

Women in the zenana know nothing of the outer world. They are trained to obey without question, to serve silently, and to endure privation and insult alike. Religion is made the cloak for the tyranny practiced upon them. (*A Princess's Pilgrimage* 52)

I, being a ruler and yet a woman, feel this double weight of existence. Though I walk among men, power does not set me free from the criticisms heaped upon womanhood. Every step forward I take must be twice justified. (*A Princess's Pilgrimage* 98)

In *A Princess's Pilgrimage*, Nawab Sikander Begum provides a stark and unflinching account of the subjugation of women in 19th-century Indian society. Through her observations, she highlights the deep-rooted ignorance and marginalization imposed on women, describing them as 'mere chattels' denied education, autonomy, or public presence (*A Princess's Pilgrimage* 45). The Zenana system, emblematic of extreme seclusion, is portrayed not only as a physical space but also as a symbol of intellectual and spiritual imprisonment. Begum articulates that religion is often used as a façade to justify and perpetuate gender-based tyranny, making the condition of women doubly oppressive (*A Princess's Pilgrimage* 52). Her personal position as both a ruler and a woman underscore the paradox of authority without social freedom—where every act of agency is scrutinized and questioned (*A Princess's Pilgrimage* 98). These reflections reveal her critical consciousness of the societal mechanisms that confine women, advocating implicitly for reform and visibility.

Parkes, meanwhile, offers a different kind of reclamation. She reclaims curiosity as a legitimate form of expertise. In a world that often-dismissed women's insights as emotional or anecdotal, she insists that her daily observations that of festivals, fabrics, food, and female friendships do matter. Her knowledge isn't detached or theoretical; it's lived. It's in the way she learns Indian languages, interacts with servants, and collects objects that tell stories. Through these small acts, she carves out her own form of authority, challenging the notion that only men, or only professionals, could truly understand India:

The condition of the native women, particularly among the higher castes, struck me forcibly. They are surrounded by wealth, but cloistered and watched with more vigilance than the jewels they wear. Their lives are ornamented cages. (*Wanderings of a Pilgrim* 103)

> A Mahomedan lady seldom appears in public, and when she does, it is under a thick veil, beneath which she can scarce breathe. Her individuality is swallowed up in her husband's identity. She owns neither opinion nor presence in the social eye. (*Wanderings of a Pilgrim* 176)

In the zenana, the life of a woman is still and monotonous. She has no part in society, no occupation save embroidery and idle gossip, and no voice in matters even concerning her own welfare. (*Wanderings of a Pilgrim* 231)

Fanny Parkes, in *Wanderings of a Pilgrim in Search of the Picturesque*, offers a colonial outsider's perspective on the status of Indian women, emphasizing their ornamental yet constrained existence. She notes the paradox of privilege and powerlessness among upper-caste women, who, despite material wealth, are "cloistered and watched with more vigilance than the jewels they wear" (*Wanderings of a Pilgrim* 103). Parkes is particularly critical of how Muslim women are denied public visibility, their identity entirely subsumed under that of their husbands, with the veil acting as both a physical and symbolic barrier (*Wanderings of a Pilgrim* 176). Her portrayal of the zenana is one of suffocating stagnation, where women are stripped of any meaningful engagement with the world beyond embroidery and idle chatter (*Wanderings of a Pilgrim* 231). While her view may carry traces of colonial paternalism, it nevertheless underscores the systemic exclusion and disempowerment of women in traditional Indian society, reinforcing the need for female agency and reform.

One of the most powerful tools in shaping identity is language. Both Begum and Parkes are acutely aware of how language frames perception. Parkes often uses a poetic, almost lyrical style that draws readers in emotionally. Her writing isn't just descriptive—it's immersive. She uses metaphor and sensory detail to paint vivid pictures of Indian life, inviting her British audience to see beyond the stereotypes of the 'mysterious Orient.' This style, while occasionally slipping into exoticism, also humanizes her subjects and reflects her desire to understand rather than dominate.

Sikander Begum's voice, though filtered through a translator, still carries authority. Her style is direct and sharp. She doesn't indulge in ornamentation; she speaks plainly and often critically. Her words feel measured, calculated, and strategic. This clarity gives her power. It allows her to speak as a reformer, as someone who sees the flaws in the systems around her and isn't afraid to point them out. Even when critiquing Meccan authorities or the state of public sanitation, she does so with the tone of someone who believes improvement is possible and who sees herself as part of that solution.

What's remarkable is how both women use language to navigate their unique positionalities. Parkes, as an outsider with insider access, blends warmth and wonder with occasional critiques. Sikander, as a sovereign subject within colonial India, mixes reverence with reformist critique. Both understand that writing is not just about storytelling, it's about shaping how readers perceive the world and, by extension, how they perceive the writer herself.

The journeys of Begum and Parkes were not just about reaching Mecca or wandering across India. They were transformative experiences, moments of personal redefinition. For Sikander, the Hajj was more than a religious obligation; it was a statement of independence, resilience, and modernity. Her observations show a woman who is fully present not just spiritually, but politically and socially. She's not content with passive worship; she questions, critiques, and reflects deeply. Her identity, therefore, isn't fixed in tradition it evolves as she travels.

Parkes, too, undergoes a transformation. Her time in India changes how she sees the world and herself. By stepping outside of her role as a British colonial wife and engaging directly with Indian life, she begins to redefine what it means to be a woman in the empire. The India she encounters is not just a backdrop; it's a teacher. Through its rituals, its people, its contradictions, she begins to find a new version of herself. In many ways, she leaves India not just with artefacts and memories, but with a renewed sense of purpose and possibility.

Travel, in this sense, becomes an internal journey as much as an external one. Both women discover parts of themselves that would likely have remained dormant if they had stayed confined to their original roles. And through writing, they crystallize these discoveries, turning experience into narrative, and narrative into identity.

Chapter II

Emergence of Women Travel Writings

"Women have always been travellers. What has changed is their ability to write about it, be published, and be remembered."

- **Birkett**

During the last twenty years, women's travel writing has moved definitively into the foreground of the Romantic literary landscape, and critical work has opened up global vistas onto women's experience during this period. Although still under-represented in modern editions in comparison to their Victorian counterparts, the primary texts are becoming more widely available, in traditional book format and through electronic resources like *Eighteenth-Century Collections Online* and Google Books. It is now feasible to research and write on the material, even teach it to undergraduates in a way that was simply not possible two decades ago. Before 1770, only two travel narratives by British women were published: Elizabeth Justice's *A Voyage to Russia* in 1739, and Mary Wortley Montagu's so-called *Embassy Letters* in 1763. Relative peace in Europe after 1763 (at least until the French Revolution), coupled with improved roads and transportation, encouraged a rise in middle-class tourism, which in turn generated an increasing number of travel narratives. By 1800, around twenty women had published travel books. (Bear in mind, however, that several hundred travelogues by men were published during the eighteenth century.) Between 1800 and 1830, 25 to 30 more women started writing about their travels. The question is what made them realise that they have to do so.

The rise of the woman travel writer in the eighteenth and nineteenth centuries has been well documented and much investigated in recent years. The 1980s witnessed several pioneering anthologies of women's early travel writing, amply demonstrating an extensive female tradition in what many had assumed to be an overwhelmingly—perhaps inherently—masculine genre. Early anthologies include: Leo Hamalian, ed., *Ladies on the Loose: Women Travellers of the Eighteenth and Nineteenth Centuries* (London: Dodd, Mead, 1981); Mary Russell, ed., *The Blessings of a Good, Thick Skirt* (London: Collins, 1988); Dea Birkett, ed., *Spinsters Abroad: Victorian Lady Explorers* (Oxford: Blackwell, 1989); Jane Robinson, ed., *Unsuitable for Ladies: An Anthology of Women Travellers*(Oxford: Oxford UP, 1994); and Mary Morris and Larry O'Connor, eds., *The Virago Book of Women Travellers* (London: Virago, 1996). More recent, and far more nuanced in its interpretive frameworks, is Shirley Foster and Sara Mills, eds., *An Anthology of Women›s Travel Writing* (Manchester: Manchester UP, 2002). View all notes The 1990s then saw a wave of seminal literary-critical and theoretical work on this topic by Sara Mills, Mary Louise Pratt and many more.

This sustained attention to eighteenth and nineteenth century women›s travel writing has not only extended our knowledge, but also greatly nuanced our understanding of women›s contribution to the genre. Some of the more simplistic assumptions originally pertaining to this material have been overturned or significantly qualified. The early stereotype was of a few eccentrics, exceptional 'spinsters abroad', overtly rebelling against the gender constraints of Georgian and Victorian society; this has given way to recognition of the many women travellers across the period, the diverse contexts in which they travelled, and the variety of modes, itineraries and attitudes they espoused. The rather utopian hope, in the first wave of feminist recovery, that women might be innately opposed to imperialism and more sympathetic than men to colonialism›s victims, has been largely disproved; yet a series of adroit analyses has simultaneously demonstrated how the hierarchies of empire were undoubtedly more fraught and complex for women to negotiate, by virtue of their being (in Indira Ghose's influential formulation) at once 'colonized by gender, but colonizers by race'.

Another reason why women chose travel writing during the colonialism is to rise their voice through writing their experiences. Women during that period were not given the privilege to speak. Rather they were kept inside the room to do the house-hold chores. Rather than assuming that women will invariably travel, and recount their travels, in a fundamentally different way from men, scholars now recognize that an individual›s experience and representation of travel is shaped by multiple, intersectional factors, including not only gender, but also race, age, class and financial position, education, political ideals and historical period. These variables will often be shared with male writers; in many contexts, accordingly, it is important to emphasize not so much the differences as the affinities and parallels between male- and female-authored travelogues. Yet whatever the similarities between men and women in these regards, women travel writers were undoubtedly often received and treated differently by editors, publishers, reviewers and readers. Frequently pigeonholed under the patronizing label of 'lady traveller', women faced satire or outright censure if they appeared to overstep the norms of contemporary femininity. Travel writing also provided empowerment to women during the colonial period.

An awareness that this might be their fate consequently informed many women›s writings up of their travel experiences, dictating the topics they addressed and prompting—to a greater extent than in male travel writers—strategies of irony, self-deprecation and what is sometimes dubbed the 'modesty topos'. So, while few scholars now recognize essential differences between male and female travel writers, most acknowledge that cultural constraints exercised a powerful shaping influence on women›s accounts, generating a degree of de facto difference from male-authored narratives and justifying today some consideration of women›s travel writing as a distinct strand within the genre as a whole.

The tradition of travel writing has, for much of literary history, borne the weight of male dominance—explorers, ethnographers, conquerors, and missionaries whose records defined the 'known' world. Yet, embedded in this tradition lies a quieter, often overlooked narrative: the story of women travellers who, against societal expectations and gender constraints, journeyed across unfamiliar terrains and chronicled their experiences. Their writings, far from being marginal curiosities, offer rich counter-narratives that interrogate the gendered dimensions of space, knowledge, and power.

The emergence of women travel writers was neither linear nor uniform. It was a patchwork of scattered beginnings, slow assertions, and occasional recognitions. From early pilgrims like Egeria and Margery Kempe to 19th-century imperial observers like Isabella Bird and Mary Kingsley, the trajectory of women›s travel writing reveals not just how women moved through the world but how they inscribed themselves into it. These narratives are shaped as much by constraints as by curiosities, and their literary strategies often mirror the negotiations these women undertook in public and private life.

This chapter seeks to explore the historical, cultural, and ideological conditions that enabled and constrained the emergence of women travel writers. It traces the roots of their narratives, the motives behind their journeys, and the shifting politics of authorship and audience. It also analyses how these narratives contest, reinforce, or complicate imperial, religious, and gender discourses.

In antiquity and the medieval period, few women had the means—or permission—to document their travels. Movement, particularly long-distance travel, was largely restricted to men, often justified through war, diplomacy, trade, or pilgrimage. Women's movement, by contrast, was tightly regulated, framed either as domestic duty or spiritual retreat.

Egeria's *Itinerarium*, written in the 4th century CE, remains one of the earliest examples of women's travel writing. Her account of pilgrimage to the Holy Land, written in a style both pious and curious, exemplifies how early Christian women navigated the tension between spiritual devotion and intellectual observation. Margery Kempe, in her 15th-century autobiography, provides another glimpse of a female pilgrim whose voice defied both gender and religious orthodoxy. Her blend of visionary experience and detailed descriptions of Jerusalem foregrounds the interplay between physical movement and internal transformation.

These texts, however exceptional, were shaped by the constraints of their time. They reflect journeys allowed and legitimized only under the aegis of religion, often needing male scribes to transcribe or validate the experience. Nevertheless, they reveal an emerging template for how women could use travel to carve out space for spiritual authority and self-expression.

With the Renaissance and Enlightenment came increased opportunities for elite women to travel—primarily as companions on diplomatic missions or through marriage alliances. As empires expanded and knowledge became increasingly secularized, travel emerged not only as necessity but also as a form of cultural capital. For aristocratic women, letter-writing and journals became outlets for intellectual engagement, even as they remained confined to the private sphere.

Lady Mary Wortley Montagu, often hailed as the progenitor of modern women's travel writing, used her time in the Ottoman Empire (1716–18) to observe, record, and challenge European perceptions of the East. Her *Turkish Embassy Letters* debunked stereotypes about the harem, praising Ottoman women's autonomy, privacy, and fashion. In doing so, Montagu resisted the masculinist lens of Orientalism and posited a proto-feminist critique of her own society.

Elizabeth Craven, Catherine Wilmot, and Mary Wollstonecraft followed with similar efforts—each using travel as a lens to analyse politics, gender, and emotion.

Wollstonecraft's *Letters from Norway* (1796), written in the wake of heartbreak, combines romantic introspection with philosophical musings. Travel, for these women, became both a literal and metaphorical journey toward self-definition.

The 19th century marked a turning point in the history of women's travel writing. Empire, railways, and print capitalism combined to facilitate and publicize the journeys of European women across Asia, Africa, and the Americas. The Victorian era, often paradoxically puritan and expansionist, created an ideological space in which upper-class white women could both uphold and critique imperial ideologies.

- This period saw the rise of prolific women travellers like:
- **Isabella Bird**, who journeyed across the American West, Japan, and Tibet, challenging male adventurers in stamina and scope.
- **Mary Kingsley**, whose scientific and anthropological observations in West Africa defied both gender and racial hierarchies.

Flora Tristan, whose journeys in Latin America were shaped by her feminist and socialist politics.

For these women, travel was not merely escapism. It was a strategy to resist domestic confinement, to access public discourse, and to establish intellectual legitimacy. Yet, as scholars such as Sara Mills and Indira Ghose have shown, these narratives are never free from the colonial gaze. They often replicate racial hierarchies even as they challenge gender norms. Bird's accounts of India and the Zenana reflect both admiration and condescension—a duality that defines much of colonial women's travel writing.

One of the fundamental challenges for early women travel writers was not travel itself—but authorship. The act of writing, and more so publishing, was a gendered transgression. Women who wrote about their travels risked being labelled as immodest, attention-seeking, or 'unnatural.' They had to justify their journeys and their narratives—often through prefaces that apologized for their boldness or emphasized their piety.

Mary Louise Pratt's concept of the 'contact zone' is useful here. Women travellers occupied this space not as dominant imperial agents but as hybrid observers—shaped by class, race, and gender. Their narratives reflect a constant tension between asserting authority and adhering to decorum. This is evident in the epistolary structure of many travelogues, the frequent invocation of religion, and the careful balancing of praise and critique.

Moreover, many women had their works edited—or filtered—by male publishers, spouses, or translators. Nawab Sikander Begum's *A Princess's Pilgrimage* (1870), while deeply authoritative, was translated and mediated by a British confidante. This raises questions about voice, agency, and audience—questions that remain central to postcolonial feminist literary criticism.

While much of the scholarship has focused on white European women, the late 19th and early 20th centuries also witnessed the emergence of women travel writers from colonized regions. These narratives are especially significant for their ability to write back—not only against patriarchy but also against empire.

Sikander Begum of Bhopal, as discussed earlier, was both a ruler and a traveller. Her pilgrimage to Mecca, documented in detail, resists both Orientalist fantasy and British paternalism. Her critique of Arabian society, her reflections on governance, and her command over multiple audiences (British and Indian) reflect a savvy negotiation of identity and power.

Later, African and Asian women such as Rokeya Sakhawat Hossain, Sarojini Naidu, and Pandita Ramabai began to document their travels—often tied to education, religion, or activism. These narratives, though less known, reveal the agency of non-European women in crafting global modernities.

In the 20th century, with wars, revolutions, and decolonization, women's travel writing underwent a significant transformation. No longer tethered only to the colonial enterprise, travel became a site for resistance, memory, and self-fashioning.

Freya Stark wrote about the Middle East with both geopolitical awareness and lyrical style. Jan Morris, as a trans woman, brought new dimensions of gender and identity into the genre. Postcolonial women writers—such as Fatima Mernissi, Arundhati Roy, or Tsitsi Dangarembga—have used travel both literally and metaphorically to address hybridity, exile, and belonging.

Digital media has further democratized travel writing. Women now blog, vlog, and podcast their journeys—transforming the travelogue from a print-based elite form into a participatory, multimedia genre. This shift not only challenges publishing gatekeepers but also widens the representation of race, sexuality, and ability in travel narratives.

To study the emergence of women, travel writers is not to recover a "lost" tradition—it is to understand how literature has always been a battleground for visibility, mobility, and voice. Women have always travelled, but their ability to write, be published, and be taken seriously has been a hard-won struggle.

Their narratives are not only about foreign lands—they are about inner journeys, identity formations, cross-cultural dialogues, and political critiques. They show us how the world was seen from the margins, how power was navigated through prose, and how women claimed space—in both literal and literary senses.

In the context of this study, the travelogues of Fanny Parkes and Nawab Sikander Begum stand as pillars of this tradition. One British, one Indian; one Christian, one Muslim; one colonizer, one colonized—yet both women used travel to speak, to document, to transform. Their legacies remind us that the map of literature is incomplete without the footsteps of women.

Chapter III

Travel Writing as Semi-autobiographical Novel

"In blending fact with personal narrative, the travelogue transcends simple documentation—it becomes a mirror where the writer sees fragments of herself reflected in every foreign land she describes." - **Singh 52**

Travel writing examines real-life, published accounts of popular eighteenth-century travellers as a novel form of creative autobiography in which lived experience is translated as narrative experiment. As a subset of life-writing, the travelogue provides the occasion for authors to self-fashion their identities as traveling subjects and attempt to reconcile their personal and national identities with constant exposure to foreign customs and modes of thought. I argue that figurative and literal landscapes in eighteenth-century travel accounts function as a crucial site for the mediation of narrative identity, enabling the internal contestations of the evolving self to be enacted upon a global stage. The experience of traveling simultaneously constructs and destabilizes the voyager's sense of 'self' and personal identity. Often, the dialectical making and unmaking of the self is mirrored in the accounts that these travellers composed and is revealed at moments when conventional plots and perceptions give way to narrative rupture, at moments when narrative voices multiply or collapse. The multiplication or bifurcation of the self is a crucial element of the travel narrative as a genre, just as it is in autobiographical genres at large. This ravelling and unravelling of the self are particularly fascinating in those texts that undertake most strenuously to represent the 'outward' self as unified, stable, and organic. The efforts these writers make to collapse the distance between the personal self and the speaking author are frequently occasions for innovative experiments in that impossible straining for autobiographical realism. While important generic differences exist between travel writing and autobiography—perhaps most importantly that the auto biographer writes to an audience that is often first the self and only secondarily other, while the travel writer, though employing the 'I,' typically writes for a public audience—autobiographical theory stresses that all representation of the self, like memory itself, is selective, self-censoring, and constructed, an effort to impose the fiction of narrative unity and coherence on our lives and on the lives of others. Thus, any account purporting to offer a complete truth about an 'elsewhere' must be treated as the product of a traveling, writing 'self,' one with a constructed narrative point-of-view. This has particular implications for how we understand the autobiographical and self-replicating strategies of narrative, including travel narrative, employed by writers located for reasons of race, class, gender, or sexual orientation outside majority culture. For Kinglake, the task is to balance one's personal impressions and feelings with the responsibility of the writer to give what he calls some true ideas of the country through which one passes. He defines his traveller in the following terms: "His very selfishness-his habit of referring the whole external world to his own sensations... You may find yourself slowly and faintly impressed with the realities of Eastern Travel" (Kinglake 112).

Kinglake is talking about himself here, of course, and if we start to compare different travel writers, what is apparent straight away is not the homogeneity of the genre but the enormous difference between the writers. So, it is true that every genre is the continuation of the other genre. Without over-lapping the genre, it should go hand in hand as travelogues and autobiographies.

The books chosen for this research also possess the same as discussed above. Begum in her travelogue is seen discussing about herself as well. She describes about Mecca as well as the surroundings of it, still in between she shares her experiences of her administration in between of the description of Arab's administration. It shows that her travelogue is not merely a travelogue but an amalgamation of two or more genres. Fanny Parkes also does the same thing as done by Begum. She was the wife of a British writer, which helped her to roam and collect the views of Indian women. She was not only wandering the area but was also pointing the things that are illegal. Travelogue is something in which one writes about the seen. But Parkes wrote about the suggestions too. She was so amazed by Indian women that she adopted some of their qualities that she decided to follow once she gets into her home town. British author Thurbon doesn't see experience, at least within the context of travel, as an intellectual endeavour or a way to learn or to gather knowledge; instead, he stresses that emotions all the important element of travel. The function of contemporary travel literature, as Thurbon sees it, is to gather not knowledge but personal experience, relating the genre's personal nature to the genre of autobiography. Outside autobiography, travel literature is the only genre that invites the first-person singular. Thubron locates the traveller within the setting, acting not as an observer but as a participant. Subsuming private thoughts and experiences within the narrative highlights the presence of the traveller for the reader and the subjectivity of the account being relayed to them. And we can see the above discussed in my selected research topic. Both the travelogues are justified with travel writing still it has some traces of autobiography also. Travel writing is about the travel experiences on undergoes, but if private thoughts and conclusions etc. comes in between it goes into the sub-genre of semi-autobiography. The travelogues discussed in this research holds the same. Both the travelogues somewhere discuss about the social issues. They obstruct it, they react against it, which shows their personal experiences. In this way, we can consider a travelogue as semi-autobiography.

    The above instances show how a travelogue can also be considered as autobiography of the author.

    Travel writing as a literary form has always occupied an ambiguous space between fact and fiction, between the personal and the observational. When a traveller narrates their journey, they are not merely reporting what they saw, but interpreting it—filtering the world through the lens of memory, identity, and emotion. This process inevitably turns even the most factual travelogue into a reflection of the self. In many ways, every travel account is a form of life writing, a semi-autobiographical mirror through which the writer constructs not just a world, but also a self.

In the context of women's travel writing, particularly during the colonial period, this autobiographical tendency takes on profound political and personal dimensions. For women travellers like Nawab Sikander Begum and Fanny Parkes, to write about travel was to insert themselves into a genre—and a world—that had long excluded them. Their texts, though ostensibly about external journeys, double as interior explorations. They are not traditional autobiographies, yet they disclose personal reflections, identity crises, ideological positions, and evolving selfhoods. They are semi-autobiographical novels in spirit, if not in form—works that encode the author's life into the narrative of the journey.

This chapter examines *A Princess's Pilgrimage* and *Wanderings of a Pilgrim in Search of the Picturesque* as semi-autobiographical travel narratives. It interrogates how both women use the travelogue not only to describe landscapes and cultures, but to chronicle their own processes of becoming—becoming a ruler, a woman of knowledge, an outsider-insider, and above all, a writer with authority.

The term 'semi-autobiographical' implies a hybrid form—part factual account, part self-construction. It is not the overt confessional mode of the full autobiography, nor the complete detachment of third-person reportage. Rather, it inhabits a liminal space where the personal seeps into the observational, and the observational becomes a vehicle for self-reflection. This blend is particularly pronounced in travel writing, where the act of moving through unfamiliar geographies often precipitates moments of internal reckoning.

Critics such as Paul Fussell and Mary Louise Pratt

have emphasized the transformative power of travel—the way in which journeys unsettle identities and provoke narrative self-fashioning. Pratt's concept of the 'contact zone' is especially useful here: the travel writer is not a neutral observer but a participant in an unequal encounter, where cultural, gendered, and political hierarchies come into play. In such zones, the self becomes unstable, multiple, and performative. And it is this performance of the self, embedded in descriptions of others, that marks the semi-autobiographical nature of travel writing.

Moreover, the female travel writer during the colonial era had to negotiate her selfhood within overlapping discourses of femininity, race, and empire. Her text was not merely a record of external events but a site for negotiating her place in the world—a place often denied to her by patriarchal and colonial structures. Thus, writing about travel became a way of writing the self into history, literature, and public consciousness.

Nawab Sikander Begum's *A Princess's Pilgrimage* is, on the surface, a pious account of her journey to Mecca. But to read it merely as a religious text would be to miss its deeper autobiographical pulse. As a Muslim woman monarch in a colonized land, Sikander's identity was doubly marked by difference—gender and race, piety and power. Her decision to undertake the Hajj, and more significantly, to publish an English account of it, reflects a strategic self-fashioning. She is not merely a pilgrim; she is a modern Muslim sovereign writing herself into a colonial narrative that sought to erase or domesticate figures like her.

The semi-autobiographical elements of the text emerge in several ways. First, there is the narrative voice—measured, authoritative, yet tinged with personal sentiment. Sikander's commentary on the sanitary conditions of Mecca, the customs of Arabian women, and the administrative shortcomings she observes are not random asides; they are expressions of a ruler's perspective, one who is deeply invested in governance, reform, and progress. In critiquing what she sees, she reveals her own political ideals and aspirations for modernity, thus giving us access to her interior world.

Second, there is the issue of textual mediation. The English version of the book was translated and edited by Mrs. Willoughby-Osborne, a British confidant of the Begum. This adds a layer of complexity to Sikander's narrative voice. While it may have been shaped for a colonial readership, the substance of the text remains hers—a negotiation of voice and agency within imperial structures. In this way, the text becomes a kind of palimpsest: beneath the diplomatic tone lies a self-conscious assertion of identity, both as a Muslim and a monarch, in a world determined to marginalize both.

Third, the illustrations and descriptions of herself in the text—rare for Muslim women's narratives of the time—signal a conscious engagement with self-representation. To insert her photograph in a travel narrative, to describe her thoughts about governance and reform, to criticize religious leaders—these are all acts of autobiographical authorship. They show a woman who refuses invisibility, who travels not only through space but into textual history.

Fanny Parkes' *Wanderings of a Pilgrim in Search of the Picturesque* is a sprawling, eclectic, and deeply personal account of her years in colonial India. Unlike Sikander Begum, Parkes was not born into power; her authority derives from experience, curiosity, and the act of writing itself. Her travelogue is marked by a sense of discovery— not just of India, but of herself. The 'picturesque' in her title may seem to refer to aesthetic landscapes, but it is also a metaphor for self-perception. Through the act of looking, she comes to understand her own desires, biases, and identity.

Parkes' text is semi-autobiographical in both structure and style. It includes journal entries, letters, recipes, sketches, and anecdotes, all woven into a narrative that resists strict genre classification. What emerges is a portrait of a woman negotiating multiple roles: wife, explorer, linguist, collector, writer. Her emotional reactions—delight, discomfort, fascination—punctuate the text, turning the journey into a personal odyssey.

One of the most striking aspects of her writing is her deep engagement with Indian women. Unlike male colonial writers who could only speculate about the zenana, Parkes gained access to these private worlds. Her descriptions of Indian women are rich, empathetic, and often admiring. These encounters serve as mirrors for Parkes' own sense of womanhood—she identifies, contrasts, and sometimes idealizes, but always reflects. In these moments, the travelogue becomes autobiographical—not because she talks about herself, but because she uses others to think through her own position in a complex colonial world.

Moreover, Parkes' collecting practices—her acquisition of Indian artefacts, art, and textiles—reveal a desire not just to possess, but to preserve. Her writing, too, is a kind of collecting: of impressions, dialogues, and cultural fragments. This curatorial impulse is autobiographical, a way of creating a life through the things and people she encounters. When she writes about her departure from India, surrounded by "the monsters and curiosities" she has gathered, it is clear that these objects are extensions of self. They are the physical remnants of a life transformed by travel.

Both Sikander and Parkes employ narrative strategies that blur the lines between fact and fiction, history and imagination. Their travelogues are not fictional in the traditional sense, but they are certainly constructed, curated, and often dramatized for effect. This performative aspect of writing is what links them to the semi-autobiographical novel.

In *A Princess's Pilgrimage*, the staging of events, the careful articulation of opinions, and the rhetorical flourishes point to a narrative crafted with intention. Sikander is not just telling a story; she is shaping a persona. She is writing herself as a modern, enlightened Muslim leader, capable of critiquing and reforming her society.

In *Wanderings*, Parkes does something similar, though with a different tone. Her humour, irony, and vivid detail often create scenes that feel more novelistic than documentary. She is keenly aware of her audience and often anticipates their questions, their scepticism, even their amusement. In doing so, she writes not just about India, but about how a British woman in India might think, feel, and evolve.

These strategies—selection, emphasis, commentary—are all part of the autobiographical impulse. They turn the travelogue into a site of self-invention. The journey becomes a metaphor for self-discovery, and the text becomes a testament to that journey.

In reading *A Princess's Pilgrimage* and *Wanderings of a Pilgrim in Search of the Picturesque* as semi-autobiographical novels, we uncover not only the personal stakes of travel writing but its political and cultural implications. These are not just stories of where the women went; they are stories of who they became through the act of writing about it.

Sikander Begum uses her travel to Mecca as a way

to articulate a modern Islamic identity, one that is loyal to faith yet open to reform, critical yet devout. Her text is a subtle assertion of Muslim female agency in a colonial world that sought to deny it.

Fanny Parkes, on the other hand, writes herself into colonial India not as a conqueror, but as a curious guest. Her admiration for Indian culture, her emotional candour, and her attention to women's lives make her text a rich site of cross-cultural reflection and self-inquiry.

Together, these texts challenge the idea that travel writing is impersonal or merely descriptive. They reveal how women, through the very act of movement and narration, could construct new selves, resist dominant ideologies, and leave behind records not just of the world, but of their place within it.

To travel is to move through the world; to write about it is to move through the self. In the hands of women like Sikander Begum and Fanny Parkes, the travelogue becomes a novel of becoming—an autobiographical narrative in which the road is both destination and transformation.

Chapter IV

Misleading Titles

"A title is part of the text—it frames it, it defines the angle of vision. A misleading title is not a lie, but a trap: it invites a reading that it then subverts." - **Eco 8**

You all have probably run into dozens of times: you click on an interesting article headline only to be taken to content that doesn't exactly fulfil the headline's promise. Even long-standing and reputable publishers have started using misleading headlines to get traffic. Now, a new study shows that these misleading titles can have more of an effect on a reader's interpretation of a book than the text in the book itself, after the whole book is written.

The Australian study, published in the Journal of Experimental Psychology: Applied, gave participants four articles to read - two factual pieces and two opinion pieces, all of which were 400 words or less. The articles also presented different slants in their headlines. For example, one of the factual pieces concerned burglary rates, which had decreased by 10 percent in the past decade but showed a 0.2 percent rise in the last year. Readers read two articles on this topic, one titled "Number of Burglaries Going Up" and one called "Downward Trend in Burglary Rate." When

93

the study participants faced a surprise quiz after reading the articles, they were better at recalling information that was congruous with the headline. In other words, readers could remember more details about the declining trend in the article titled "Downward Trend..." while also having better retention of the 0.2 percent increase in the article titled "Number of Burglaries Going Up." The headlines told readers what to focus on, and those are exactly the details they retained. On the other hand, most readers were able to infer that the burglary rate would decrease next year regardless of article headlines.

In the opinion pieces, however, both inference and retention were skewed due to misleading headlines. Readers were presented with a piece about genetically modified food. The article contained contrasting information from an expert and a layperson, the food expert stating that GM foods are safe and the layperson expressing concerns. Some participants read the article under the title "GM foods are safe," while others saw the headline "GM foods may pose long-term health risks." Despite reading the same exact article, participants were found to side with whatever slant the title took. Readers of "GM foods may pose..." were also more willing to pay extra money for organic food in the future. The main problem here is that publishers are posting articles with lofty headlines that generate clicks but end up actually leaving readers with skewed versions of the truth. This happens even if the whole article is read. Thus, the study suggests that content creators are doing a serious disservice to their readers by using headlines such as these. The question is this: if publishers and article writers know that readers retain information from the headline more than anything else in the article, don't they have a responsibility to avoid headlines that bend the truth? Can readers be blamed for not examining content more closely and getting to the true crux of a story?

Now same things are happening in books as well as in travelogues too. Have you ever picked up a book based on its title and after reading the synopsis or first few pages realized it wasn't about what you'd hoped for? Of course you have, because misleading book titles are a problem all book lovers will come to face in their lifetime. While there are some outrageously horrible titles out in the world, misleading titles aren't necessarily bad, they just don't convey the message of the book as clearly as one would hope. And don't get me started on misleading book covers, because that's an entirely different ball game.

There are plenty of moments where we must have picked up a book based on the title and gotten excited about it, only to realize my excitement was misleading. Sometimes this works out for the better, like in middle school when we were first handed *To Kill a Mockingbird* and rolled my eyes while all the boys in class cheered thinking it would be about hunting and killing. The title of a book is important, but some title miss the mark by a long shot. Many classics have some odd titles, as do newly published books. Misleading titles will probably never cease to exist, so it's important that one shouldn't judge a book by its title (or cover). You never know, a crazy title might lead you to a remarkable story. As these travelogues did to us when we started reading them. Begum's *A Princess's Pilgrimage* shows the truth of the Arab society where Muslims go for *Hajj*. Also, it empowers women. The book also shows how in the colonized society also a woman was daring to write. However, the title suggests us a very healthy pilgrimage done by a princess, but everything turned into ashes when we go inside and read the whole travelogue. The whole travelogue is very interesting giving us ideas to know the reality of the pilgrimage. According to her, one must not heighten the facts until facing the situation. She beautifully presented the truth behind the veil. Parkes' *Wanderings of a Pilgrim* also has the same case. The title suggests some good pictures of the surrounding, nature's beauty etc. but it consists if the harsh realities of Indian women in *Xenana*. Where women suffer at the utmost level. Parkes' wife of a British writer supports Indian women to provide them with identity and respect which they deserve. It shows how we are told that it is a travelogue where the pilgrim roams but through these wandering messages are delivered to women as well as audience: "Even as a woman and a ruler, I was subject to the scrutiny of strangers" (Begum 84).

While going through Begum's travelogue we can note that a princess going for pilgrimage will continue with scenic beauty and some pious truth about God will come out but it doesn't hold true. Rather than providing us with knowledge of Hajj, she goes on describing the faults of the pious place that no one ever dared to show. Anyone who will read the title however, will think about all good things. But she empowered herself as well as the women of India to speak truth and stand by it. Pilgrimage/ pilgrim just plays a role in title but as we move forward the books will provide us with many turnings. We cannot say that Parkes and Begum are deceiving us but rather we can say the social issues that they have put up in their travelogues are very hard to describe during the colonial period. They must have used the title to avoid any discrepancies in their publication of books. We can say that sometimes misleading titles are not bad, we get knowledge and also get empowerment through it. The empowerment that we are talking about is discussed in the next chapter.

Titles are often the first words a reader encounters: *"The title is not a label. It is a lens"* (Atwood 42). They act as a gateway, a promise, a provocation. In the context of travel writing, particularly women's travel writing from the colonial period—titles carry the burden of expectation. They do not merely describe; they construct. They shape perceptions even before a reader delves into the narrative, positioning the work within specific ideological, cultural, and literary frameworks. The two texts under study in this book, *A Princess's Pilgrimage* by Nawab Sikander Begum and *Wanderings of a Pilgrim in Search of the Picturesque* by Fanny Parkes are no exceptions. At first glance, their titles appear straightforward, even poetic. But upon closer inspection, they are layered with ironies, contradictions, and misdirection that merit critical unpacking.

This chapter examines how these titles, rather than being transparent indicators of content, are sites of tension. They both reveal and conceal, seduce and distract. They reflect the authors' identities, their narrative strategies, and their negotiations with empire, gender, and genre. By analysing these titles closely, we can better understand the rhetorical and political choices embedded within the texts themselves:

The Muhammadan community in India has so degenerated that many of its customs are diametrically opposed to the tenets of Islam. One sees strange innovations at every step, and the true spirit of religion is lost in outward show. My journey to the Hejaz revealed to me the curious ways in which even the sacred pilgrimage is corrupted by ignorance and petty rivalries among the pilgrims. (Begum 114)

This quote is important because it shifts the reader's attention from an exotic royal journey (as the title might imply) to a pointed critique of religious and social practices:

My presence here as a female sovereign is a matter of some curiosity to the local Arab population. But I carry the firman of the British Government, and that lends a certain authority to my person. Still, I cannot help but feel that I am under constant observation, as if a native ruler must always justify her place—more so if she be a woman. (Begum 89)

This exposes the underlying theme of surveillance and gendered governance, clashing with the romantic expectations a reader may form from the title.

In any literary tradition, a title serves as a framing device. In travel writing, it does even more—it anchors a geographic, cultural, and psychological journey. Titles in this genre typically aim to entice curiosity, assert authority, or suggest a sense of adventure. For male authors, titles such as *Travels into the Interior of Africa* or *Voyages and Discoveries in the South Seas* offered a claim to territory, both literal and literary. For women, however, the stakes were different. Their titles often had to negotiate the same tensions their texts did: the balance between decorum and daring, observation and opinion, submission and subjectivity.

Women travel writers were expected to be modest in both voice and visibility. Their titles were often carefully chosen to downplay the act of transgression that travel itself represented. A title, then, could be a mask—a way to soften the radicalness of a woman journeying alone, writing publicly, or criticizing social norms.

At first blush, the title *A Princess's Pilgrimage* evokes humility, devotion, and femininity. It conjures images of a royal woman, perhaps cloaked in modesty, embarking on a journey of spiritual significance. The term 'pilgrimage' carries religious and emotional weight. It suggests a quest for purity, enlightenment, or redemption. 'Princess,' meanwhile, implies grace, privilege, and sheltered upbringing.

However, the actual content of Nawab Sikander Begum's travelogue defies these expectations at every turn.

Sikander Begum was not merely a princess. She was the ruler of Bhopal—a sovereign, a stateswoman, and an administrator. By framing her Hajj as 'a pilgrimage,' the title diminishes the broader implications of her journey. This was not simply a spiritual undertaking. It was a performance of power, a statement of autonomy, and an exercise in imperial diplomacy. Her journey was conducted with grandeur, involving hundreds in her entourage, and included detailed observations on governance, infrastructure, and hygiene—hardly the content of a typical religious pilgrimage.

Moreover, the title omits any indication of the colonial entanglements underlying the text. The fact that the travelogue was translated and edited by a British woman, Mrs. Willoughby-Osborne, for an English audience, complicates its authorship and authenticity. The title does not hint at this mediation, nor does it prepare the reader for the layers of surveillance, negotiation, and cultural translation that characterize the text.

In calling it a 'pilgrimage,' the title assumes a narrative of piety. Yet Sikander Begum's tone is often pragmatic, even acerbic. She critiques the conditions of Meccan society, the inefficiencies of religious leadership, and the unsanitary living conditions. These are not the expected devotions of a pilgrim but the evaluations of a ruler. Her gaze is more administrative than reverential.

The term 'pilgrimage' also traditionally connotes personal spiritual transformation. But in Sikander's narrative, the transformation is less about faith and more about self-representation. She uses the pilgrimage to construct herself as a modern, enlightened Muslim monarch—a figure at once faithful and reformist. Thus, the title misleads by suggesting a conventional narrative of inner awakening when it is actually a highly political and performative act.

Fanny Parkes' title is longer, more lyrical, and seemingly romantic. It promises the reader a leisurely, perhaps whimsical, account of travels through exotic lands in pursuit of beauty. The word 'wanderings' suggests aimlessness, perhaps even innocence. 'Pilgrim' adds a touch of spirituality or moral weight. And 'picturesque'—a heavily aestheticized term of 19th-century sensibility—evokes romantic landscapes, ruins, and sublimity:

I often visited the zenana, and the conversation would turn to matters of childbirth, superstitions, and the practice of seclusion. These women, cloaked in their veils, spoke with such clarity and intelligence about the world that it astonished me. They, who rarely stepped beyond the walls, held within them a knowledge passed from mother to daughter like sacred lore. (Parkes 273)

This passage complicates the supposed aim of the book, 'the picturesque', by shifting attention to ethnographic depth and gender studies: "The English gentlemen who come to India often see only what flatters their sense of superiority. They speak of progress, while the lands they manage lie barren, and the people grow restive. I have found myself more at ease among villagers than among those who carry the flag." (Parkes 418)

This critical note departs from the light-hearted wanderings implied by the title and instead delves into colonial power dynamics. But like Sikander's title, this one also misrepresents or rather, selectively frames, what the book is truly about.

To search for the 'picturesque' in colonial India is not an apolitical act. The picturesque, as a visual and literary mode, was a way for Europeans to aestheticize and domesticate the unfamiliar. Ruins, poverty, and exotic customs could be appreciated from a safe distance—as objects of curiosity rather than subjects of understanding. In promising a search for the picturesque, Parkes signals an imperial gaze, even if unintentionally.

Yet, her actual text is far more complex. Parkes is not merely gazing; she is engaging. She learns Indian languages, adopts Indian customs, and enters the private world of Indian women. Her 'wanderings' are not directionless but deeply intentional, often aimed at understanding the people she lives among. She critiques aspects of both Indian and British society. She reflects on colonial injustices even while benefiting from her position within empire.

In this light, the title's invocation of the picturesque seems reductive. It belies the ethnographic, philosophical, and emotional depth of the work. It promises scenery but delivers society. It offers aestheticism but unveils anthropology.

Like Sikander, Parkes adopts the term 'pilgrim.' But what kind of pilgrimage is this? Parkes' quest is neither spiritual nor religious in the conventional sense. It is, at best, a metaphorical pilgrimage—a journey of self-discovery and cultural immersion. Yet even this metaphor is unstable.

Unlike the traditional pilgrim who humbles herself before the sacred, Parkes often assumes the role of a mediator or interpreter. She lectures the reader, catalogues Indian customs, and constructs meaning for a metropolitan audience. She may empathize with India, but she also exoticizes it. Her pilgrimage, if it can be called that, is shaped more by curiosity and collection than by reverence or repentance.

The title thus misleads by invoking a tradition of humility and faith, when the actual text oscillates between curiosity, critique, and cultural conquest.

Why do these misleading titles matter? The answer lies in the power of representation. Titles frame the narrative before it begins. They precondition the reader's expectations. In doing so, they can subtly sanitize, sensationalize, or simplify what is to come.

In the case of *A Princess's Pilgrimage*, the title neutralizes a bold political act by cloaking it in religiosity and femininity. It reinscribes the writer within the conventional roles of pious womanhood, even as her text challenges that very norm. In *Wanderings of a Pilgrim in Search of the Picturesque*, the title romanticizes colonial travel, masking its complexities with aesthetic longing.

This misdirection is not accidental. They are strategic—reflecting the authors' own negotiations with gender, genre, and audience. In an era where women were discouraged from travel and public authorship, both Sikander and Parkes had to tread carefully. Their titles, like their narratives, are works of artful diplomacy.

To call these titles 'misleading' may, in fact, be

to undersell their ingenuity. Perhaps a better term is 'multivalent.' They operate on multiple registers. They are at once sincere and ironic, descriptive and deceptive, conventional and subversive.

Sikander's 'pilgrimage' is not only to Mecca but to political subjecthood. Parkes' 'picturesque' is not only visual but philosophical. Both titles, then, act as decoys and declarations—inviting readers into a narrative space that is richer and more rebellious than the titles let on.

This complexity is precisely what makes these works valuable today. They remind us that travel is never just about movement. It is about meaning. And meaning, especially in the hands of women negotiating empire, patriarchy, and authorship, is always slippery.

Titles are not simply marketing tools. They are ideological constructs. They shape what is seen and what remains hidden. In the case of *A Princess's Pilgrimage* and *Wanderings of a Pilgrim in Search of the Picturesque*, the titles are both revealing and concealing. They echo the constraints under which these women wrote and the strategies they deployed to assert agency within those constraints.

Titles, though brief, are powerful literary tools. They serve not only as invitations into a text but also as frameworks for interpretation. For centuries, the function of titles has evolved—from straightforward descriptions to layered devices that shape and even manipulate the reader's expectations. In the realm of travel writing, titles often carry the weight of geographical, cultural, and philosophical signposts. When placed in the context of women's travelogues during the colonial period, however, titles become more than just literary labels; they become instruments of negotiation, concealment, subversion, and empowerment.

In this chapter, we have examined the seemingly simple titles of two influential travelogues: Nawab Sikander Begum's *A Princess's Pilgrimage* and Fanny Parkes' *Wanderings of a Pilgrim in Search of the Picturesque*. On the surface, both titles appear to align with conventional genres—religious travel in the former, and aesthetic or touristic exploration in the latter. Yet, as the detailed analysis of their content reveals, both texts stretch far beyond the boundaries suggested by their titles. This conclusion unpacks the implications of these titles further, arguing that they are deliberately 'misleading' in ways that reflect the broader constraints and creative strategies available to women writers in the 19th century. These titles function not merely as representations of the texts but as coded responses to societal expectations, gender norms, and colonial power structures.

Titles as Concessions: Negotiating the Space to Speak

It is essential to understand that both Begum and Parkes were writing within male-dominated and politically charged environments. The act of women authoring travelogues itself was subversive, and more so when the narratives critiqued religious, cultural, or colonial systems. Given these constraints, the use of strategic titles can be seen as a necessary literary compromise—a means of gaining entry into the public sphere without triggering immediate backlash.

In this context, *A Princess's Pilgrimage* functions as a title that cloaks the political weight of the narrative beneath a veneer of piety and personal devotion. It signals a spiritual journey—an acceptable and even expected form of travel for a Muslim woman in the 19th century. Yet what unfolds in the text is not merely a record of religious fulfilment, but a comprehensive critique of the administrative inefficiencies of Mecca, a reflection on the condition of women in Islamic society, and a subtle alignment with British ideals of governance and reform. The title, therefore, acts as a soft front, allowing the author to explore themes of modernity, sovereignty, and self-definition under the guise of religious duty.

Similarly, Fanny Parkes' *Wanderings of a Pilgrim in Search of the Picturesque* draws upon the popular 19th-century trope of the 'picturesque' to frame her travels in India. The picturesque, as understood in the context of British aesthetic theory, was associated with beauty, harmony, and exotic landscapes—an ideal that often masked colonial objectification and appropriation. By invoking this trope in the title, Parkes positions her work within a safe and familiar genre, one that would appeal to British readers interested in India's visual allure. Yet, once the reader delves into the text, it becomes apparent that Parkes is not merely 'wandering' or passively consuming aesthetic experiences. Rather, she is actively engaging with Indian society, learning languages, entering domestic spaces like the zenana, and expressing critiques of both British and Indian social structures. Her 'pilgrimage' becomes an intellectual and emotional exploration; far deeper than the aesthetic mission her title suggests.

The Politics of Disguise: Strategic Misrepresentation as Subversion

These titles can thus be read as acts of strategic misrepresentation—a form of literary camouflage that enabled these women to navigate a world that was not entirely ready for their voices. In this sense, the titles are not misleading in a simplistic or deceptive way, but rather perform a complex function: they conceal in order to reveal, they comply in order to critique.

This strategy is reminiscent of what feminist scholar Judith Butler describes as 'performativity'—the idea that identity is constructed through repeated performances that both reinforce and subvert norms. In titling their works as they did, both Begum and Parkes are performing identities that align with socially acceptable roles: the devout princess, the romantic pilgrim. But once inside the narrative, these performances are destabilized. The devout princess turns out to be a reformist critic; the romantic pilgrim becomes a cultural mediator and proto-ethnographer. The titles thus allow entry into discourse while creating the space to undermine it from within.

This tactic can also be read through the lens of Homi Bhabha's concept of mimicry in postcolonial theory. Bhabha argues that colonized subjects often mimic the colonizer's ways not to assimilate fully, but to subtly subvert the authority of colonial power. Begum's use of English, British administrative logic, and royal authority in her narrative mirrors this idea. Her title, echoing a devotional genre that would be palatable to both Muslim and colonial sensibilities, allows her to articulate radical critiques under a veil of conformity.

Similarly, Parkes' picturesque wanderings, while seemingly emulating the colonial gaze, actually reconfigure it. Her careful attention to Indian women, rituals, and everyday life challenges the detached superiority typically found in male colonial travelogues. Thus, the title's mimicry of a known trope enables a reworking of that very trope, offering a more humanized, gendered, and complex view of colonial interaction.

Gendered Framing: Titles as Markers of Female Mobility

In both cases, the titles serve not only as literary devices but as gendered statements. Travel, particularly in the 19th century, was coded as a male domain—a realm of conquest, science, diplomacy, or adventure. For women to enter this space required justification, often couched in terms of family duty, religious calling, or aesthetic appreciation. The titles chosen by Begum and Parkes reflect this need for justification.

For Begum, identifying herself as a 'Princess' and her journey as a 'Pilgrimage' signals a noble and spiritual purpose—one that would not raise suspicion in either Islamic or colonial patriarchies. Her identity as a ruler gives her a public voice, but her title ensures that the journey is framed within moral and religious legitimacy. Yet the irony lies in how she uses this framing to assert secular authority, criticize political systems, and position herself as a modern, enlightened leader. The title thus becomes a bridge between personal devotion and political engagement.

Parkes, in titling herself a 'Pilgrim,' appropriates a language of spiritual searching, often associated with humility and introspection. Yet her narrative reveals not only spiritual but also intellectual ambition. Her search for the picturesque becomes a search for knowledge, cultural understanding, and personal growth. The modesty implied by the term "wanderings" contrasts sharply with the purposeful, well-documented, and assertive nature of her actual travels. Again, the title functions as a strategic gender performance—disarming the reader while enabling deeper reflections on empire, culture, and identity.

Reception and Interpretation: The Long Shadow of Titles

The influence of a title does not end with its

publication; it often shapes the reception and afterlife of a text. For decades, both *A Princess's Pilgrimage* and *Wanderings of a Pilgrim* were read narrowly because of their titles. Scholars and casual readers alike approached them expecting devotional reflection and scenic commentary, respectively. As a result, the political, cultural, and feminist dimensions of these works remained underexplored for much of the 19th and 20th centuries.

It is only through contemporary critical readings—particularly feminist and postcolonial scholarship—that the full richness of these texts has been unearthed. Today, we recognize that the 'misleading' quality of these titles is precisely what makes them interesting. They reflect the constraints under which women wrote, the cleverness with which they navigated those constraints, and the enduring challenge of interpreting texts shaped by complex identities.

Titles, then, are not mere afterthoughts. They are rhetorical devices that operate within a specific historical and cultural grammar. In the case of Begum and Parkes, titles function as tools of literary strategy, allowing entry into a male-dominated genre while opening space for critique and self-representation. They are simultaneously protective and provocative—shielding their authors from censure while inviting deeper inquiry from more discerning readers.

Toward a Feminist Hermeneutic of Travel Titles

What do these insights mean for the broader study of women's travel writing? They suggest the need for a feminist hermeneutic—a reading practice attuned to the ways women's narratives are shaped not only by content but by paratextual elements like titles, prefaces, and editorial framing. Feminist theorist Shari Benstock has argued that 'women's autobiography must be read differently, because it is written differently.' The same applies to travel writing.

Titles like *A Princess's Pilgrimage* and *Wanderings of a Pilgrim in Search of the Picturesque* are not anomalies or accidents; they are deliberate acts of narrative positioning. They reveal how women authors anticipated their audiences, navigated power structures, and crafted layered identities through the act of naming. To dismiss them as simply 'misleading' is to miss their performative brilliance and political subtlety.

Moreover, by analysing these titles as performative texts in their own right, we gain a deeper appreciation of how language functions within systems of gender and power. These titles remind us that travel writing, especially by women, is never just about movement through space. It is about movement through discourse—about finding ways to speak, to be heard, and to leave a trace in a world that often prefers women's silence.

Concluding Reflections: Titles as Invitations and Interventions

Ultimately, the titles of these travelogues do more than mislead; they provoke, protect, and provoke again. They are thresholds between what is expected and what is delivered—between the visible and the concealed, the said and the unsaid. They ask the reader to step inside under certain assumptions, only to challenge those assumptions page by page.

In *A Princess's Pilgrimage*, the reader is invited into a tale of spiritual fulfilment, but leaves with a vision of political reform, cultural critique, and female agency. In *Wanderings of a Pilgrim*, one anticipates scenic detachment, but encounters emotional involvement, linguistic immersion, and anthropological curiosity. These shifts are not betrayals of the title, but expansions of its promise. They reveal that titles, like journeys, may begin in one place but end in another.

For women like Sikander Begum and Fanny Parkes, writing was not just an act of documentation—it was a form of defiance. Their titles reflect this defiance in masked form, asking us to read not only what is written, but what is implied. In recognizing the artifice and ambition behind these 'misleading' titles, we come to see these texts not as minor works in the canon of travel writing, but as foundational interventions—works that reshaped the map of who gets to travel, to speak, and to be remembered.

To read these titles critically is to unearth the deeper narratives of self-fashioning, resistance, and redefinition. It is to see how women writers, despite systemic limitations, found ways to write themselves into history—not just through content but through the very act of naming.

The titles may mislead. But the texts enlighten. And in that interplay, a new geography of female authorship emerges—one marked not by passivity or piety, but by intelligence, courage, and creative subversion.

Chapter V

Travel Writing for Women's Empowerment

"As a woman I have no country. As a woman my country is the whole world."

— **Virginia Woolf**

Empowerment through travel is not just about mobility; it is about reclaiming agency—physical, intellectual, and narrative. The act of movement becomes a metaphor for personal liberation and sociopolitical assertion. Feminist theorists such as Sara Mills, bell hooks, Gayatri Chakravorty Spivak, and Gloria Anzaldúa have all examined, in different ways, how space, language, and power intersect in women's lives. When applied to travel writing, these ideas illuminate the deeper implications of texts like *A Princess's Pilgrimage* and *Wanderings of a Pilgrim in Search of the Picturesque*.

Sara Mills' critical work on gender and travel writing outlines the discursive mechanisms that marginalize women in traditional narratives. Mills argues that "women's travel writing often has to negotiate a space within dominant male-authored paradigms, which define travel as conquest, exploration, and the claiming of the unknown" (56). Women writers, then, challenge this notion by offering counter-narratives where travel is interpreted as introspection, solidarity, and cultural engagement. This model better reflects the narratives of Parkes and Begum, who often engage with cultural others empathetically, even if filtered through their respective imperial and religious positions.

Bell hooks' idea of 'choosing the margin as a space of radical openness' also finds resonance here. Both Parkes and Begum inhabit marginal positions within the dominant narratives of empire and gender: Parkes, as a woman in the colonial structure, and Begum, as a native Muslim woman within both patriarchy and colonialism. Their texts thus reflect an effort to speak from the margins—yet not as victims. They use these margins as launching points for critique, self-expression, and alternative forms of authority.

Similarly, Anzaldúa's concept of the 'borderlands'—a space of hybridity and negotiation—helps articulate how women travellers negotiate their multiple identities. Nawab Sikander Begum's identity as a devout Muslim, a reformist ruler, and a colonial subject place her firmly in such a borderland. Her travel writing becomes a means of reconciling these identities into a coherent voice. Parkes, too, navigates a complex terrain where her appreciation for India coexists with the constraints of her British imperial upbringing. These 'borderland' texts are spaces where contradictions are acknowledged rather than erased.

Gayatri Spivak's assertion that the subaltern cannot speak is partly answered by travelogues like *A Princess's Pilgrimage*. While Spivak emphasizes the ways colonial discourse mutes native voices, Begum's narrative reveals a rare case where the subaltern not only speaks but does so with political clarity and literary competence. The mediation of her voice by Mrs. Osborne does raise questions of authenticity, but it does not erase Begum's agency altogether. In fact, the very act of translating and publishing such a voice in English during the colonial era reflects a strategic subversion of power structures.

Feminist geographers like Doreen Massey and Gillian Rose have long emphasized that space is not neutral; it is actively produced and contested. Women's travel writing, particularly in colonial contexts, reclaims space by narrating it from a gendered perspective. Massey suggests that space is 'a product of interrelations; as constituted through interactions.' In travel writing, these interactions are not just with geography, but with the self, the Other, and dominant ideologies.

Fanny Parkes' entry into spaces like the zenana disrupts both colonial and gendered geographies. The zenana, a space defined by seclusion, becomes a site of visibility and voice when described by Parkes. Her access to these traditionally private domains highlights how gendered spaces can be both preserved and reimagined. The descriptions she provides give presence to women who were usually absent from colonial records, even if her portrayals are filtered through a British lens.

In contrast, Nawab Sikander Begum's journey to Mecca reverses the gaze: a non-Western woman observing another part of the Islamic world. She scrutinizes the management of sacred spaces, local customs, and the treatment of women, creating a form of feminist geography from within an Islamic framework. She does not romanticize the journey; instead, she interrogates it with the critical eye of a ruler, a reformer, and a woman. Her writing maps a geography of accountability—where even the holy must be reformed if found unjust.

Comparative Glimpses: Parkes and Begum alongside Kingsley, Stark, and David-Néel

While Parkes and Begum are central to this study, it is valuable to place them in dialogue with other pioneering women travel writers who similarly used travel to assert intellectual and personal freedom.

Mary Kingsley is one such figure. Her travels in West Africa in the late 19th century resulted in the publication of *Travels in West Africa* (1897), where she criticized British missionary efforts and documented African customs with a degree of respect uncommon among her contemporaries. Like Parkes, she was an outsider willing to engage with cultures on their own terms, though not without her own biases. Kingsley's humour, courage, and scepticism toward colonial interference echo Parkes' nuanced stance on India. Yet unlike Parkes, Kingsley remained firmly opposed to the idea of women's suffrage, showing the contradictions even within empowered narratives.

Freya Stark, who explored the Middle East and Asia in the 20th century, often wrote about the limits of imperial perception. In *The Valleys of the Assassins* (1934), Stark criticizes the arrogance of British officials and emphasizes the complexity of Arab societies. Her writing, though coming later than Parkes or Begum, reflects a shared commitment to detailed observation and personal introspection. Stark's ability to travel largely alone and her multilingualism resonate with Begum's sovereignty and independence.

Alexandra David-Néel provides another compelling parallel. A French explorer, she travelled in disguise to enter the forbidden city of Lhasa in 1924, becoming the first European woman to do so. Her writings document not just the physical journey but also her philosophical engagement with Tibetan Buddhism. Like Begum, she defied not only gender expectations but also spiritual boundaries, challenging the dichotomy between the observer and the observed.

These women, like Parkes and Begum, turned travel into a transformative encounter—with the world and with themselves. They did not merely 'see' other cultures; they engaged, documented, critiqued, and reimagined. Their narratives collectively underscore that travel writing by women is not ancillary to the genre—it is foundational to a broader, more inclusive understanding of mobility and knowledge.

The Narrative Voice: Asserting Authority Through Style

The empowerment of women through travel writing lies not only in the act of travel but in how the journey is narrated. The control of voice, tone, and perspective becomes a form of narrative power—reclaiming space in a literary world that has long dismissed women's accounts as sentimental, secondary, or subjective. Both Nawab Sikander Begum and Fanny Parkes use distinctive narrative techniques that subvert such dismissals, instead asserting themselves as credible, intelligent, and authoritative voices.

Sikander Begum's voice in *A Princess's Pilgrimage* is laced with regal poise, political astuteness, and religious conviction. The very decision to document her Hajj in English (albeit through translation) is radical. Her text, though mediated by Mrs. Osborne, retains the sharpness of observation and intellectual critique. She does not present herself as a passive pilgrim but as an inspector of systems, a commentator on hygiene, politics, and gender norms in Mecca. For instance, she does not hesitate to describe the Arabian officials as 'corrupt and disorderly,' an opinion that would have seemed audacious from a woman — and even more so from a Muslim Indian woman under colonial surveillance. She writes with a ruler's gaze, noting inefficiencies, proposing reforms, and comparing practices to British administrative ideals. Her tone is composed but never deferential, making her writing a space of self-legitimation.

Fanny Parkes, on the other hand, adopts a more personal and informal tone in *Wanderings of a Pilgrim in Search of the Picturesque*. Her writing mixes description, anecdote, journal entries, and letters — a hybrid form that defies the rigid genre conventions of her time. This stylistic openness allows her to express emotion, curiosity, and reflection without compromising her authority. Unlike the stiff, male-authored travel reports that dominated colonial literature, Parkes' voice is warm and humane. She documents her learning process — her acquisition of Hindi, her observations of Indian rituals — not as an expert, but as a respectful learner. Yet, this self-effacing posture is deceptive: it allows her to insert critiques of British colonial attitudes while appearing apolitical.

Representing Women: A Gendered Ethnography

Both Parkes and Begum pay special attention to women in their respective narratives, offering insights into gender roles across cultural lines. What is notable is how both women challenge existing stereotypes — though not without internalizing some of their own.

In *A Princess's Pilgrimage*, Begum makes frequent references to Arabian women. She comments on their physicality, dress, behaviour, and social roles. While some of her remarks—particularly about their muscular strength or untidiness—may sound judgmental, they are more nuanced than a simple rejection. Her writing reflects an active comparison between her own notions of womanhood, informed by Indian Muslim and British administrative ideals, and what she perceives in Arabia. In doing so, she creates a layered gendered ethnography that critiques patriarchal norms across cultures, even when those norms are embedded within Islamic traditions.

Fanny Parkes' portrayal of Indian women—particularly those she met in zenanas—is equally revealing. She expresses fascination with their customs, jewellery, and domestic lives, and her accounts reflect genuine admiration. Her ability to access female-only spaces, denied to male colonial officers, allows her to construct an insider's view of Indian femininity. However, Parkes is not free from colonial exoticism. At times, her descriptions verge on the picturesque and ornamental, framing Indian women as static cultural artifacts. Nevertheless, she often distances herself from the disdainful tone of other memsahibs, choosing instead to depict Indian women as dignified, intelligent, and capable of deep affection and resilience.

Importantly, both women humanize their subjects in a world that frequently reduced women—especially Eastern women—to tropes of victimhood or sensuality. In Parkes' writing, the zenana becomes a site of intimacy, not just oppression. In Begum's narrative, the Hajj is a site of piety and political visibility for Muslim women, not merely a religious duty.

The Politics of Language and Translation

Language itself becomes a site of empowerment—

and contestation—in both travelogues. For Nawab Sikander Begum, writing in English (through translation) was both a necessity and a strategic move. It ensured a wider readership, particularly among the British administrative elite, allowing her to assert her political and moral intelligence. However, this choice also subjects her narrative to colonial interpretation. Mrs. Osborne's role as translator/editor inevitably influences tone and emphasis. Yet, Begum's ideas remain clear. Her critique of Meccan governance and emphasis on reform transcend translation. Her use of English becomes a double-edged sword: a tool for visibility and a mechanism of soft control.

Parkes, on the other hand, uses English to bridge cultures. Her attempts to understand Hindi and Sanskrit reflect a desire to connect linguistically, though the text remains entirely in English. The structure of her sentences, often peppered with Indian terms and idioms, shows a hybridization of linguistic forms. This blending is significant—it mirrors her own ambivalence about empire and her deep (though sometimes idealized) admiration for Indian society.

Language, then, in both narratives, is not just a medium—it is a method. Through translation and code-switching, Begum and Parkes negotiate their positions as both insiders and outsiders, both observers and participants.

Travel as Intellectual and Emotional Empowerment

Another axis along which empowerment unfolds in these travelogues is the intellectual autonomy and emotional agency they afford their authors. Travel provides both Begum and Parkes with a platform to reflect on their roles as women, to critique systems of power, and to reimagine their identities.

Begum uses her Hajj not only to fulfil a religious obligation but to express political views, propose reforms, and assert her capacity as a modern sovereign. Her writing reflects deep concern for public health, administrative efficiency, and women's welfare—issues often excluded from male-authored hajj narratives. The pilgrimage becomes a metaphor for her vision of a modern Islam— one that is spiritually devout, socially progressive, and politically aware.

Parkes' emotional connection to India is a form of resistance to the detachment expected of colonial agents. Her descriptions of Indian music, festivals, and religious practices show genuine enchantment. She finds joy in learning, pride in discovery, and melancholy in departure. These emotional registers—often dismissed as feminine or sentimental—are actually subversive. They validate a different kind of knowledge production—one rooted in affect, intimacy, and lived experience.

Visuality, Collection, and the Colonial Gaze

One of the most interesting aspects of Parkes' travelogue is her collection of Indian artefacts, which she took back to Britain. Her collection served not just as memorabilia but as a material extension of her narrative. Through it, she participated in the production of colonial knowledge, albeit in a more personalized and gendered form. The display of these objects in metropolitan settings gave her legitimacy in male-dominated circles of collectors and scholars.

However, this act also implicates her in the colonial gaze—the act of seeing, possessing, and displaying the 'Other.' While Parkes' collection stems from admiration, it also transforms Indian culture into aestheticized objects for Western consumption. This dual role—both curator and colonizer—underscores the tensions in her empowerment.

Begum, by contrast, does not collect objects. Instead, she collects *observations*. Her power lies not in displaying the Orient but in interpreting it. Her gaze is critical, reformist, and grounded in shared religious identity. If Parkes' collection represents colonial fascination, Begum's critique represents postcolonial introspection. Both forms, however, assert female agency: one through possession, the other through interpretation.

Legacy and Afterlife: Reception, Canonization, and Silences

The immediate reception of *A Princess's Pilgrimage* and *Wanderings of a Pilgrim in Search of the Picturesque* was marked by ambivalence. While both texts were published and read during their authors' lifetimes, they were often marginalized in literary and academic canons for decades. It is only in recent years, through the efforts of feminist, postcolonial, and travel literature scholars, that these works have been re-examined and revalorized as complex, valuable documents of female experience and expression.

Sikander Begum's work, for instance, was long considered an oddity—a rare instance of a Muslim woman writing during the colonial period. Her status as a princely ruler and her English publication led some early readers to dismiss the text as an elite anomaly, not representative of broader female experience. However, scholars such as Siobhan Lambert-Hurley and Barbara Metcalf have helped recast the travelogue as a sophisticated negotiation of power, gender, and identity. Today, Begum's work is viewed as a pioneering effort in Muslim women's life writing and as an early example of indigenous critique within colonial modernity.

Similarly, Fanny Parkes' *Wanderings* was read primarily as a curiosity or a colonial souvenir. Only recently has her travelogue been recognized as a nuanced and rich ethnographic account that complicates binary views of colonizer and colonized. Her work now finds its place in critical anthologies of women's travel writing and postcolonial literature, cited as a unique example of British empathy and engagement with Indian culture in a period marked by detachment and condescension.

The delayed recognition of these texts reflects broader patterns of exclusion in literary history—where women's voices, especially those that defy easy categorization, are either ignored or misinterpreted. Their canonization today is not just a correction of literary oversight; it is a political act that reclaims silenced narratives and re-centres alternative epistemologies.

Contemporary Relevance: Feminism, Mobility, and Decolonial Thought

The relevance of Parkes and Begum's travelogues extends far beyond their 19th-century contexts. In the 21st century, where questions of gender, migration, cultural hybridity, and narrative agency are once again urgent, these texts offer valuable insights.

First, both authors exemplify how mobility can be a mode of empowerment. At a time when women's movements are still policed—through laws, surveillance, and cultural expectations—Parkes and Begum remind us that to move freely, to see, and to speak, remains a radical act. Their journeys were not just physical; they were epistemological revolutions, asserting that women can be observers, interpreters, and narrators of the world.

Second, their texts embody early forms of what

we now call *intersectional feminism*. Both authors navigate multiple identities—Begum as a Muslim, a monarch, and a colonial subject; Parkes as a woman, a wife, and a semi-insider within imperial India. Their reflections resist simplistic binaries. They demonstrate how empowerment is not absolute but negotiated, contextual, and multi-layered. These narratives affirm that feminism must be situated— attuned to history, location, class, race, and religion.

Third, their work resonates with decolonial feminist thought, which seeks to dismantle Eurocentric norms of knowledge and representation. Begum's text, though shaped by colonial mediation, challenges Orientalist fantasies by offering a Muslim woman's view of sacred space, governance, and society. Parkes' narrative, while situated within imperial privilege, complicates British superiority by honouring Indian aesthetics, rituals, and resilience. These travelogues resist the homogenizing gaze of empire and instead foreground plurality and empathy.

In our current age, marked by debates over immigration, religious identity, cultural appropriation, and postcolonial reparations, Parkes and Begum offer models of how to engage with the 'Other'—not through domination or romanticism, but through attentive witnessing and honest self-reflection.

Beyond the Texts: Travel as a Feminist Praxis

Both travelogues exemplify how writing about journeys can become a practice of world-making. Travel writing, particularly by women, is not merely about where one goes; it is about how one makes sense of movement, difference, and selfhood. Through their narratives, Parkes and Begum transform travel from a masculine conquest into a feminist praxis.

They claim space—not only on maps but on pages. Their prose, filled with detail, emotion, critique, and vision, asserts that women are not passive passengers of history but its co-creators. Travel, for them, is not escapism. It is engagement. It is a way of thinking critically about society, about belief, and about the fragile boundaries between cultures.

This shift—from passive witnessing to active storytelling—is the true mark of empowerment. Through their writings, both women offer testimony: not just of the places they saw, but of the selves they became through the act of travel. Their works remind us that narrative is itself a form of mobility—a way to cross borders, resist containment, and arrive at new understandings of the world and one's place in it.

Final Thoughts: Writing Back, Writing Forward

In reading *A Princess's Pilgrimage* and *Wanderings of a Pilgrim in Search of the Picturesque*, one is struck by how much these women anticipated future debates in feminist, postcolonial, and travel theory. They wrote back—to the empire, to patriarchy, to expectation. And in doing so, they wrote forward—paving paths for later generations of women to speak, to move, and to author their own lives.

These travelogues are not relics. They are living documents—full of questions, provocations, and insights that remain unfinished. They challenge us to ask: What does it mean to see? To be seen? To narrate? Who gets to move—and who gets to write about movement? And how can the stories we tell about travel help shape a more just, inclusive, and empathetic world?

As this chapter has shown, the power of travel writing lies not only in where one goes, but in how one transforms the journey into a declaration of selfhood. For Nawab Sikander Begum and Fanny Parkes, travel was not merely an activity—it was a political and literary intervention. It was a way of saying: I was here. I saw. I thought. I wrote. I mattered.

In reclaiming their voices, we reclaim a tradition of feminist writing that insists on dignity, complexity, and the freedom to move.

Empowerment can be defined as a multi-dimensional social process that helps people gain control over their own lives. Women's empowerment refers to "women's ability to make strategic life choices where that ability had been previously denied them" (Malhotra et al., 29). Accordingly, empowerment is central to the processes of maintaining the benefits of women at an individual, household, community and broader levels (Malhotra et al., 9). It involves the action of boosting the status of women through literacy, education, training and raising awareness (Alvarez and Lopez, 13). Hence, women's empowerment is all about allowing and equipping women to make life-determining choices across different issues in the country. We all know the ratio of girls is less as compared to boys in our country, India. And it is due to the orthodox mentality of society who wants to have boys and not girls. In true sense, patriarchy has decided the course of women's lives throughout ages.

The need for women empowerment arose because of the gender discrimination and male domination in the Indian society since ancient time. Women are being suppressed by their family members and society for many reasons. They have been targeted for many types of violence and discriminatory practices by the male members of the family and society in India and other countries as well. Wrong and old practices in the society from ancient times have taken the form of well-developed customs and traditions.

Women enjoyed a better position in the Rig-Vedic period which deteriorated in the Vedic civilization. Vedic civilization onwards, women were denied the right to education, right to widow remarriage, right to inheritance and ownership of property.

Social evils like child marriage and dowry system worsen the situations more for women. During the Gupta period, the status of women deteriorated extremely and institutions like dowry and Sati Pratha became more prominent.

During the British Raj, many social reformers such as Raja Ram Mohan Roy, Ishwar Chandra Vidyasagar, and Jyotirao Phule started agitations for the empowerment of women and as a result of their efforts Sati was finally abolished and the Widow Remarriage Act was formulated.

Later, stalwarts like Mahatma Gandhi and Pt. Jawaharlal Nehru advocated women rights and as a result of their concentrated efforts that the status of women in social, economic and political life began to elevate in the Indian society. Although women in India have made a considerable progress in the seven-decade of Independence still the battle is only half won.

They still have to fight against many social evils that are oppressing them and deteriorating their status. Still, there are people or groups that create hurdles and resists women progress in India. In India, women have always been a victim of honour killings. They have been bereft of basic rights for proper education and freedom for years. In this male-dominated and patriarchal society, they face violence, abuse and other ill-treatment. All the evil practices that are deteriorating the status of women need to eliminate from our society if we really want to empower women of our nation. Gender inequality still prevails in India because of which women are maltreated not only by outsiders but by family members too. And, we all know that women are strong as hell—especially women in travel. Despite still facing so much economic and social inequality worldwide, women still travel the world and are making a huge impact as students, volunteers, teachers, and adventurers abroad. This shows their empowerment. In Nawab Sikander Begum's book a minor community Muslim woman roaming around and giving advices are something unusual during the colonial period. She became the pioneer for all the women to roam, analyse and write. The analysis of every particular things during the *Hajj* requires courage to speak and write too. Through her writings she is providing women empowerment to speak out and to proof themselves as one of a kind. In Fanny Parkes' travelogue also, there are act giving women the empowerment to take stand for themselves. She started collecting ideas about Indian women and their well-being. After knowing about *Zenana*, she revolted against the total idea. She also protested the act of *Sati* and condemned the total act. She took some good qualities of Indian women with her, which in a way empowered Indian women by making them realise that they also possess qualities which is adored by European women. It can be noticed that *Wanderings* helped her to present herself to the public on her return to Britain. Alongside, the travelogue also looks to the objects she collected and how she in turn curated these for audiences in Britain in the mid-nineteenth century. When she returned to the metropole this research argues, her writings and collection lent her authority in an almost exclusively masculine society of Indian 'experts'. She gained entrée to a social world to which she might not otherwise have been admitted and formed a life independent of her own life. On returning to Britain then, she publicly utilized her collection to validate and enhance her experiences. It also shows how a woman linked to East India Company was able to use her experiences of the subcontinent to effect on return. These are the advantages that women could garner. The above shows how Fanny used her experiences for empowerment of herself as well as for all women during that period. In the period of male-dominated world collecting as well as status and many independences in the metropolitan society holds in the top most level during that period. She took lessons in Hindi and Sanskrit and started to explore the intricacies of Indian culture. In particular, she also became very anxious to witness the lives of the high-class Indian women kept in seclusion behind its closed doors i.e. the *harem*. Her detailed and valuable knowledge of another culture and her understanding of its social world- particularly that of the *Zenana*, a world closed to men gave her status in a metropolitan, masculine society. She struggled a lot to bring recognition for Indian women. She made women realise that the things done to them is not the right thing. Through direct or indirect way empowerment is given to women. In Begum's *A Princesses' Pilgrimage* empowerment is given in another way, being from a Minority Muslim community stood as the queen of Bhopal. She ruled Bhopal and managed the administrative part very well. She went for pilgrimage but didn't point out the as usual positives. She pointed out the harsh realities of Mecca. She pointed out the women of Mecca. Another feature of Arabian society that garnered the especial attention of the ruling Begam were the sanitary arrangement. She came back and wrote the travelogue which itself acted as an empowerment for women.

Travel is not merely the act of moving through space; it is an odyssey of transformation. For women, especially in eras dominated by rigid patriarchal norms, travel has often meant more than reaching a destination— it has meant reclaiming agency, voice, and vision in a world that had long dictated how far they could go and what they could say. Travel writing, then, is not just about documenting the exterior world; it becomes a site of self-assertion, a proclamation of existence.

In the 19th century, women like Nawab Sikander Begum and Fanny Parkes did what few dared: they wrote. Not just in diaries tucked away in drawers, but in books, in public, under their own names. They challenged the assumptions of the time—that woman belonged to the domestic sphere, that their thoughts lacked intellectual value, and that their experiences were secondary to those of men. Through their travelogues, these women disrupted the dominant narratives and carved a literary space that was at once personal, political, and deeply empowering.

This chapter explores how travel writing functioned as a powerful tool for women's empowerment during the colonial era and beyond. It draws upon the lived journeys and written testimonies of Parkes and Begum, showing how their travelogues opened new avenues of self-expression, challenged imperial and patriarchal constructs, and continue to inspire reimagining of identity, freedom, and authorship.

In an age when decorum dictated that a woman's place was in the home, to set foot into foreign lands was already a subversive act. For Nawab Sikander Begum, travelling to Mecca was not only a religious pilgrimage but a declaration that Muslim women could—and should—participate in public religious life. Her detailed documentation of the journey, composed in a voice that is often witty, critical, and incisive, asserts that women have the capacity to observe, analyse, and articulate complex sociopolitical realities.

Similarly, Fanny Parkes, the wife of a British civil servant, immersed herself in Indian life in a way that defied the expected aloofness of British memsahibs. She rode horses across dusty Indian plains, visited temples, spoke local languages, and wrote with an intimacy and curiosity that made her an outsider among her own people. Her writing was not just about documenting landscapes—it was about redefining what a woman could see, do, and understand.

In both cases, travel writing became a vehicle of rebellion. By moving physically through forbidden spaces, these women also crossed symbolic boundaries—of gender roles, racial assumptions, and colonial hierarchies.

The power of travel writing lies not only in the movement it documents, but in the voice it constructs. For women who were long silenced or filtered through male narration, the act of writing itself was revolutionary. It offered a means to define the self, to own one's perspective, and to leave behind a trace—a permanent mark in a world where they were often rendered invisible.

In A Princess's Pilgrimage, Sikander Begum does not merely recount the logistics of her Hajj. She reflects on sanitation systems, criticises administrative inefficiencies, and observes cultural practices with the analytical sharpness of a reformist. Her voice, though translated and mediated through Mrs. Willoughby-Osborne, cuts through with authority and presence. She is not a passive narrator. She is a ruler, a reformer, a writer.

Parkes, on the other hand, is more personal, even poetic. Her Wanderings of a Pilgrim in Search of the Picturesque is filled with emotional observations, sketches, recipes, and letters. Her narrative is sprawling and layered—part journal, part memoir, part political reflection. In a society that often-dismissed women's emotions as irrational, Parkes elevates them into valid modes of knowing and experiencing the world.

Their writings show that the personal is indeed political. By narrating their experiences, these women claim authorship not just of texts, but of selves.

One of the most striking features of women's travel writing is the way it reclaims the right to look, to interpret, and to explain. In traditional travel narratives, especially those by colonial men, the world is a passive object to be described and categorized. The gaze is unidirectional—white, male, imperial.

But in the hands of writers like Begum and Parkes, the gaze is complicated and contested.

Sikander Begum, as a Muslim woman ruler, writes about Mecca and Medina not as distant Oriental sites but as spaces she inhabits, critiques, and reflects upon. Her gaze is both internal and external, religious and political. She refuses to romanticize Arabia and is candid about its flaws. In doing so, she subtly subverts the exoticism common in Western accounts of the East.

Parkes, meanwhile, offers a counter-gaze. She does not view Indian women as mere subjects of pity or exotic wonder; she interacts with them, learns from them, and describes them in their full humanity. Though not free from colonial prejudice, her writing attempts empathy and curiosity rather than dominance.

Through their eyes, readers are introduced to

alternative cartographies—maps drawn by women, not of conquest, but of encounter, of listening, of questioning.

Empowerment through travel writing must also be understood in relation to the intersecting forces of gender and empire. Both Begum and Parkes navigate complex terrains—not only geographical but ideological.

Begum, despite her royal status, operates within the limits imposed by British colonial rule. Her writing is shaped by the need to appeal to an English-speaking audience, yet she manages to critique Arabian society and portray her own Muslim identity with dignity and intellect. Her dual marginalization—as a woman and a colonized subject—makes her authorship all the more remarkable.

Parkes, though British, is marginalized within the colonial framework because of her gender. Her refusal to conform to the passive role of the memsahib brings both criticism and admiration. She gains access to zenanas and religious rituals that were off-limits to British men, turning her gender into a form of epistemic advantage.

In both narratives, empowerment is not absolute— it is negotiated, fragile, and complex. But it is real.

Women travel writers often became inadvertent advocates. By describing the lives of those they encountered, they humanized cultures that were otherwise reduced to caricature by colonial discourse.

Parkes' sympathetic portrayal of Indian customs— though occasionally tinted with exoticism—helps to counterbalance more hostile British representations of India. Her admiration for Indian music, textiles, architecture, and social rituals presents a version of India that is not just a colony, but a civilization.

Sikander Begum, by criticizing the inefficiencies of Mecca's administration, positions herself not only as a devout pilgrim but as a forward-thinking ruler. She becomes a cultural mediator—translating Muslim life for British readers while advocating for reform within her own tradition.

This dual function of the travel writer—as observer and advocate—is one of the ways in which travel writing enabled women to participate in broader political and intellectual conversations.

The influence of women's travel writing extends far beyond literature. It reshaped how societies thought about women, knowledge, and authority.

By publishing their experiences, Parkes and Begum set precedents. They made it possible for future women—like Freya Stark, Alexandra David-Neel, and even contemporary travel writers—to speak publicly about their journeys. They also provided alternative models of heroism: not the conqueror, but the connector; not the warrior, but the witness.

Moreover, their works continue to serve as rich sources for historians, feminists, postcolonial scholars, and students seeking to understand how gender, travel, and power intersect.

Their writing invites us to rethink what it means to 'know' a place, to 'observe' a culture, and to 'write' a life.

Travel writing gave women like Nawab Sikander Begum and Fanny Parkes more than an audience. It gave them a voice; a voice that could not be confined by veils or corsets, by imperial rule or gender roles. In their words, we find maps not just of geography, but of liberation.

Their stories teach us that travel can be a form of resistance, that writing can be a declaration of freedom, and that empowerment does not always come with fanfare—

it sometimes comes with quiet reflection, with a pen, and with the courage to describe the world as one sees it.

In a world still marked by borders and biases, their legacy reminds us that to travel, and to write, is to refuse silence.

Chapter VI

Women's Travel Writing as Resistance and Cultural Translation

"Travel is more than the seeing of sights; it is a change that goes on, deep and permanent, in the ideas of living."
— **Miriam Beard**

Women's travel writing during the nineteenth century did more than document journeys and foreign lands; it forged a radical space where gender, power, and narrative intersected to redefine who could speak, what could be seen, and how it could be interpreted. The travelogues of Nawab Sikander Begum and Fanny Parkes stand as powerful examples of this literary insurgency. Though shaped by different cultural, political, and religious frameworks, their writings act as both resistance to dominant narratives and as acts of cultural translation. Through observation, critique, and immersion, these two women challenged the imperial male gaze and the constraints of feminine decorum, each in her own way.

This chapter explores how both *A Princess's*

Pilgrimage and *Wanderings of a Pilgrim in Search of the Picturesque* reflect modes of resistance to hegemonic structures and function as bridges between worlds. It draws attention to how these women mediated between the personal and political, between local and global, and between imperial and subaltern voices. In doing so, their texts become sites where cultural boundaries are negotiated and historical narratives are rewritten.

Narrative as Resistance: Breaking the Silence

In colonial contexts, writing was a privileged act. For women, especially, it was doubly transgressive: to travel was to leave the domestic space, and to write about that travel was to claim intellectual authority. Nawab Sikander Begum, a Muslim ruler from Bhopal, and Fanny Parkes, a British expatriate in India, both occupy unusual positions in this regard. Their gendered identities, far from being impediments, become lenses through which they reinterpret power, culture, and space.

Sikander Begum's decision to undertake the Hajj and publish her reflections in English was extraordinary. Her account, though filtered through the colonial translation of Mrs. Willoughby-Osborne, remains assertively critical and self-aware. Her travel to Mecca, a religiously charged destination largely inaccessible to outsiders, already defied prevailing norms for Muslim women. However, by documenting her impressions of governance, hygiene, and gender roles in the holy cities, Sikander Begum resists the idealization of Mecca and offers instead a candid, at times critical, portrayal. This critique is not anti-Islamic but reformist, positioning her as a rational moderniser.

Fanny Parkes, on the other hand, resists the stereotype of the aloof memsahib by embedding herself within Indian life. Her travelogue is an eclectic mix of curiosity, affection, and occasional critique. Rather than positioning herself as an expert or superior observer, she often writes with the awe and humility of someone who sees herself as a student of the culture she inhabits. In a period when colonial ideologies were consolidating themselves, Parkes' tone is, by comparison, iconoclastic. She embraces the sensory, emotional, and spiritual dimensions of Indian life, allowing her text to become a site of cultural intimacy.

Both women resist reductive representations—Parkes of the "Orient" and Sikander Begum of the Islamic world. By foregrounding their individual experiences, they rupture dominant paradigms of colonial travel writing that tend to generalize, exoticize, or silence.

Translating Cultures: Writing Between Worlds

Cultural translation is not merely a linguistic act; it is an epistemological and political one. Both travelogues demonstrate how women authors could act as intermediaries between cultures, even as they grappled with the limits of their positionalities.

Sikander Begum's *A Princess's Pilgrimage* is a rich example of cultural translation on multiple levels. First, there is the literal act of translation—her Urdu narrative rendered into English by a British woman. But beyond this, her account is carefully calibrated to speak to both Indian and British readers. Her praise for British administrative efficiency contrasts with her scathing remarks on Meccan officials, and her analysis of Arabian women reflects both admiration and disappointment. This dual address reflects a political astuteness: she constructs herself as a loyal British ally while simultaneously asserting the moral and administrative authority of her own rule. In essence, she is translating her experience of Mecca into a narrative that affirms her identity as both a devout Muslim and a modernising sovereign.

Fanny Parkes also engages in cultural translation, but in the reverse direction. Her writings aim to demystify India for British audiences. She incorporates translations of Indian songs, culinary notes, descriptions of rituals, and reflections on Hindu philosophy. In doing so, she offers her readers not just information, but interpretation. Her work functions as a bridge between India and England, fostering empathy even as it sometimes falls into orientalist tropes. Her translations are not always accurate by academic standards, but they are emotionally resonant and often driven by a desire to dignify rather than diminish.

Both writers demonstrate that translation is not neutral. It is shaped by purpose, audience, and ideology. Yet, both use it to expand rather than constrain the understanding of the 'other'. In translating their experiences, they also translate themselves—as women negotiating complex worlds.

The Politics of the Female Gaze

The 'gaze' is a central concept in postcolonial and feminist theory, often referring to how power is exercised through looking and representation. In traditional colonial literature, the gaze is male and Western; the object is female and Eastern. However, in these travelogues, the gaze is female and complex.

Sikander Begum's gaze upon the holy cities is neither passive nor reverent. It is investigative. She describes the dirt in the streets, the corruption of officials, and the behavior of Arabian women with a critical edge. Her gaze unsettles the sacredness of space and the idealisation of gender roles.

She is both insider and outsider—a Muslim in Mecca, yet a South Asian woman critiquing Arab patriarchy. This duality enriches her gaze, allowing it to be both culturally embedded and critically distanced.

Parkes' gaze, meanwhile, is marked by its intimacy and immersion. Unlike male travel writers who surveyed India from a distance—through battles, architecture, or governance—Parkes entered homes, zenanas, kitchens, and markets. Her observations often reflect a tactile, sensual engagement with Indian life. She writes about fabrics, spices, gestures, and smells—elements often dismissed as feminine or trivial, but which carry rich cultural meanings. Her gaze does not merely observe; it touches, listens, and feels.

Yet, both authors are not immune to the biases of their contexts. Sikander Begum's criticism of Arabian society sometimes echoes British colonial ideologies of reform and order. Parkes occasionally falls into the trap of exoticising Indian rituals. But what is noteworthy is that both complicate the gaze: they neither fully submit to nor fully escape dominant discourses. Their gaze is partial, plural, and situated.

Writing as Agency: Narrating the Self

Travel writing becomes, for both women, an act of self-narration. It is a genre that permits the weaving of personal, political, and philosophical threads. Both texts are deeply autobiographical, though not in the confessional mode.

Sikander Begum writes not just as a traveller but as a ruler. Her narrative choices reflect a concern with governance, law, and social reform. Her identity as a Muslim woman leader is carefully curated: she is devout but progressive, loyal but autonomous. Her writing negotiates multiple audiences and roles, offering a layered portrait of a woman who reclaims authorship in a context that often denied it.

Parkes, in contrast, writes herself as a learner and lover of India. Her travels are not heroic expeditions but lived experiences. Through her letters and sketches, she constructs a self that is curious, empathetic, and brave. Her authority is not derived from conquest or command, but from connection. Her text becomes a space where she fashions a new self—a woman of insight, cultural sensitivity, and narrative skill.

In both cases, writing is not just about recounting a journey; it is about becoming through narrative. Travel transforms them, and writing solidifies that transformation. In a world that sought to define women through silence, domesticity, or deference, these texts articulate a different possibility: of the woman as witness, critic, and author.

Dialogues Across Empire

Finally, the most powerful aspect of these travelogues is the dialogue they establish—not just between writer and reader, or self and other, but between the colonised and the coloniser, the East and the West, the sacred and the secular. Read together, *A Princess's Pilgrimage* and *Wanderings of a Pilgrim in Search of the Picturesque* offer a layered conversation.

Sikander Begum critiques Arabia in ways that might resonate with British readers, but also asserts her own vision of Islamic modernity. Parkes admires India in ways that often defy British arrogance, yet is still shaped by colonial sensibilities. Each woman is embedded in the empire but also extends beyond it. Their writings question binaries: insider vs. outsider, modern vs. traditional, coloniser vs. colonised.

Their works create a space where dialogue replaces monologue, where understanding replaces appropriation, and where complexity replaces stereotype. They do not always succeed in transcending the limitations of their contexts, but their efforts mark a significant shift in the politics of representation.

Writing Back, Writing Through

In reclaiming the right to travel and to write about it, Nawab Sikander Begum and Fanny Parkes resist multiple forms of erasure. Their travelogues are more than literary texts; they are acts of defiance, translation, and transformation. They show that women's mobility—whether across deserts or across ideas—can reshape not only how we view the world, but how we view the self.

Through narrative, they push against the boundaries of race, class, empire, and gender. They do not merely describe the world; they remake it in their image. And in doing so, they leave behind not just records of journeys past, but roadmaps for future women travellers, writers, and thinkers. Their legacy lies not only in where they went, but in how they wrote—with clarity, courage, and a commitment to truth as they saw it.

Thus, women's travel writing in the colonial period, as exemplified by these two texts, becomes a genre of possibility. It is a literature of motion and emotion, of distance and intimacy, of critique and celebration. It resists silence. It translates lives. And most importantly, it writes women into history.

Conclusion

Nowadays we are totally familiar with the image of lone female travellers, each night there are overseas reporters from the BBC and CNN, travel correspondents in exotic locations and game show hosts traipsing through thick jungles. However, even 100 years ago the sight of a lone female traveller in foreign climes raised eyebrows. Despite this, there were still adventurous women prepared to take on a challenge and discover the world for themselves. Previously many of the early female travel writers were often nuns, aristocrats or wives that kept their husbands company on foreign missions. By the nineteenth century it became more common to find women with their own fortunes, these pioneers were intent on seeking strange lands and exotic countries without accompaniment and writing about their discoveries or publishing journals along the way. One of the earliest recorded female travellers was the pilgrim Margery Kempe (1373 – 1438) whose works were only uncovered in the 1930's and tell of her travels to Rome, Spain and Jerusalem. Another early author who changed the travel writer genre was Lady Mary Wortley Montagu (1689 – 1762). Her *Turkish Embassy Letters* whilst accompanying her husband, the Ambassador in Constantinople, gave an enlightening first-hand account of the private lives of women in Islamic society. Mariana Starke (1761 – 1838) redefined travel writing and is credited with being the creator of the first true European travel guide in 1820 covering France and Italy. Previous books had dwelt principally on art and architecture, whereas Starke's book offered advice on passports, hotels, and food prices, it also included an exclamation mark rating system too. Elizabeth Cochrane aka Nellie Bly (1864 – 1922) was an investigative journalist with the New York World Newspaper. She became the first person to travel around the world in less than 80 days, while re-enacting Jules Verne's famous novel, meeting the author on route. Armed with one set of clothes, a small travel bag, £200 and a quantity of gold she set off from New York in November 1888 arriving back some 72 days later. These and many other such ladies who took risks, chances and with their articles, letters and publications helped bring a new, personal perspective to the whole genre of travel writing and in doing so opened up opportunities for others to follow in their footsteps. The above are some examples of the writers who gave directions to other women to know about the real world. The things they did during that period must be considered as a great achievement. Sarah Richardson, in an excellent study of Victorian women's political activism, comments that "women employed genre as unlikely as travel writing and domestic economy to engage their readership with the key political, economic and social issues of the time" (23). Modern travel writing might be an unlikely form to use for such discussions; eighteenth- and nineteenth-century voyages and travels were precisely the genre many readers went to, and respected, for information and commentary on these issues, as evidenced in the domestic context by the work of figures like Young and William Cobbett, and in the overseas context by the many commentaries offered by travellers on the public affairs of other nations. In misjudging travel writing's importance in the eighteenth and nineteenth centuries, then, we may undervalue the significance and influence of the work women produced in the genre. This tendency is often compounded by another, closely related misconception about the era. Recent scholarship has quite rightly emphasized what Turner terms the 'discursive heterogeneity' of women's travel writing in this period, and the opportunity the genre gave them to engage with a broad range of disciplines and discourses; Spence, for example, includes 'arts, antiquities, and history' and 'natural or historical anecdotes' among the themes a good travelogue needs to address. Yet when discussing their treatment of some of these topics—those we now regard as strongly marked as masculine domains in the eighteenth and nineteenth centuries (for example, science, politics and economics) there is a tendency to assume that women could only have been very marginal commentators on these issues, necessarily positioned outside major circuits of knowledge production and opinion formation. Thus, Kinsley comments that while travel writing encouraged women to conduct empirical investigations into many topics, 'disciplines such as aesthetics, antiquarianism, geography and science' nevertheless remained close to women at anything other than an amateur level. It is for this reason, many critics strongly imply, that women turned to travel writing as a medium to engage with these disciplines. The genre, it is assumed, let them engage with a range of wider debates under the radar, as it were, without risking the stronger and potentially more controversial assertion of authority that might come from publication of a formal treatise or study; yet, by the same token, this roundabout strategy seemingly signals the extent to which they were excluded from the principal sites and modes of discussion in these fields. Many travelogues by women possess a more complex, manifold valence than we tend to recognize today. Juggling conversational and technical idioms, mediating between public and semi-public spheres and their associated modes of communication, travel writing was a genre in which women might play a sophisticated double game, at once exhibiting yet also disclaiming authority, simultaneously speaking knowledgeably to congenial audiences while shielding themselves from attacks by chauvinist readers hostile to overt displays of female learning. This 'double-voiced' quality to women's travel writing has again long been acknowledged by critics, since at least the time of Sara Mills' seminal *Discourses of Difference* (1991). Yet discussion of this tendency has generally emphasized double voicing as a strategy of subterfuge and subversion, forced upon women by their marginalization from authoritative discourse. Less attention has been paid to its enabling aspects, and to the reception and influence of these texts among readers willing and able to appreciate the substantive information they contained. Her travel writing, and her innovative career as a whole, took shape within a more variegated literary and journalistic landscape, in which there were many public voices prepared to speak up for women's travel writing. If the *Monthly Magazine* categorized Graham as a woman of genius, the *Eclectic Review* assessed her thus:

Women are said, we think with justice, to be the best letter writers; and we should be tempted to assign to them the praise of being the best tourists, had we a few more female writers like Maria Graham to adduce in support of the assertion. Thus, there were not only important intellectual networks which welcomed women travellers and accepted contributions from them, but there were also reviewers and other public commentators who looked favourably on women's travel writing and argued for its usefulness. It is needed to be done as women travelogues provide us with that knowledge that no men travel writer can provide us. One can therefore talk of the *female gaze*, the *colonial gaze*, the *Western gaze*, etc. My aim is to set the stage for discussions of difference and to do so by using primary sources throughout the course, especially travel texts. Although there is the use of the occasional men's text for comparative purposes, on the whole the work concentrates on women's texts. This is done to emphasize women's presence throughout the timeframe of the course. They may not have been in power, but their significance was noteworthy. The masculine tradition of travel writing was considered to reflect public and professional concerns, whereas the feminine tradition was considered to fall into the private and personal sphere. Mary Kingsley's work belies this stereotype. She allied herself with the masculine tradition of producing scientific research, yet she was well aware of social expectations. She adopted a self-deprecating and humorous style to deflect criticism of inappropriate behaviour on her part.

Fanny Parkes and her husband collected a lot during their twenty-three years of residence in India. The collection of her travels in India appears to have given her a public legitimacy and authority lacking before she went to the subcontinent. India and her experiences there changed her and enabled her to construct a new identity for herself. Whatever the wandering traveller says, he does so from having seen that of which he speaks was the oriental proverb she quoted in the opening pages of *Wanderings of a Pilgrim*, emphasizing the veracity of her enterprise. 'Knowing India first-hand' was a claim frequently made by travel writers of the period when attempting to add authority to this literary aspect of the imperial project. Fanny's sense of 'knowing' was enhanced by gathering objects from the subcontinent and by sharing her acquired knowledge with a public eager to see the curiosities, the monsters and the idols' that she took with her when she left India forever. Fanny's enthusiasms appear in her own account so unfeignedly artless as she gathers people, customs and curiosities on her travels through India, that it is hard to see a conscious self-fashioning in her actions, certainly while she was living in India. Yet in writing of her collecting artless enthusiasm, Wanderings suggests that Fanny distinctly wished to be understood as someone who had formed knowledge and expertise through 'authentic' experience. With little means of corroborating the events that Parkes described in Wanderings, it is difficult to ascertain the exact nature of her experiences and the stories she told about them. Rather than work towards ascertaining such knowledge, this research instead focused on how Fanny's travelogue can be considered as a travelogue which provided identity to women, how it worked as an empowerment for women, how travelogues are considered as partial autobiographic in nature. It also analysed the way in which she sought to present herself to the public on her return to Britain. The above-mentioned things show how travel helped Fanny to come out of her boundaries that was destined for her. But somehow, she managed to get into the centre rather than staying in the periphery. She managed to know things about Zenana and also brought that into forefront. She also condemned the act of Sati. It shows her respect towards India as well as Indian women. To write things in for of India during colonial period required guts to portray. But

Fanny portrayed it in a beautiful manner. She used the title Wanderings of a Pilgrim in a two-way purpose to attract Indian as well as British audience. Indian women can take the travelogue as empowerment and British audience can take the travelogue as a way through which they can know India well. Nevertheless, focusing on Fanny Parkes as an avid collector of Indian material culture allows us to see how men and women within the company's ambit often engaged with multiple aspects of Indian society, seeking out meaningful ways of communicating with the indigenous peoples and entering with enthusiasm into the Indian Ocean World. Fanny shared her love for India with others through the journals and letters which were published as Wanderings of a Pilgrim; she painted and drew vivid scenes, which were reproduced in her book. She created a visual journey for the public with her 'Grand Moving Diorama of Hindostan'. In publishing her writings and making them available to a wider audience and in creating exhibitions from her writings and collection, Parkes self-consciously sought to use her writings and experiences to greater effect. They provided a space in which her experiences to greater effect. They provided a space in which her experiences of India and the stories she wished to tell of them could shape a broader conception of who she was and what she had achieved. Fanny's impulse to bring her memories of India, as Jasanoff would suggest, but also satisfied what Susan Stewart describes as the 'insatiable demands of nostalgia'. Her experiences and her accumulated knowledge, shared with the British public, gave her authority and status in a largely masculine area of activity. Her access to the intimate world of the exclusively female harem of high-caste Indian women and her descriptions of this offered a rare insight into an exotic world and enhanced the picture of the colonized for a fascinated metropolitan public. She turned what she had gained in India- independence, knowledge, experiences into a new life for herself in the metropole. Her expertise brought her status and legitimacy in this imperial metropolitan world. Her engagement with India may have been limited and partial in its investigations, her 'travelling gaze' to some extent blinkered by a sense of imperial entitlement and prejudice, the arrangement of objects in her Cabinet of Curiosities lacking coherence and organization, the picture she drew revealing more about colonial beliefs and behaviour than those of the subject race. But it is the energy and enthusiasm fuelling her project now brings colonial British India in all its failings and insecurities vividly to life. It shows how every aspects is justified in the research. Fanny Parkes in her travelogue has used many stances where not only travelogue is seen we can see her cry for Indian women. We can feel her desperate call for women empowerment.

Nawab Sikander Begum on the other hand justifies how a minority community Muslim women can bring changes in women's life in the colonial period. The research highlighted three main themes other than justifying objectives. First of all, it will examine the text's location within an Islamic tradition of travel writing as negotiated within a colonial context. Issues of motivation, audience, structure and style will be addressed, as well as the possible reasoning behind the book's published form. It will then seek to identify ways in which notions of the self were depicted in this narrative, questioning whether Sikander's main aim was to chart a personal journey of faith, as one may expect, or craft an identity more closely related to political concerns. This paper also turned to investigate the Begam's perception of Arabia the 'other' as an alternative construction of 'the orient'. Her travelogue will, thus, be treated as a form of ethnography in which her perspectives on gender roles, sanitation and religious practice can be revealed. And it also discussed on what can be gained in terms of our understanding of travel and travel-writing from looking at the Hajj narrative of journey that, while influenced by the colonial milieu, remained distinct from any European experience of travel. Bhopal, the state ruled by Sikander in the mid-nineteenth century, was one of nearly six hundred principalities encompassing two-fifths of the area and one-third of the population of the British Indian Empire that retained nominal independence in the colonial period. It is worth noting that, in the period before 1857, these formal treaties between the company and the 'native princes' were often abrogated a key example mentioned being that of Awadh in 1856 on the basis of administrative inefficiency or the lack of a natural male heir. This way Sikander became the princess of Bhopal. Her mother Qudsia was also a great administrator. The women of their family had it in their blood to be one of a kind. Sikander has also been celebrated by her descendants on account of being the first Indian ruler, male or female, from the most powerful emperor down to the smallest chieftain, to make the pilgrimage to Mecca. Even the greatest of the great Mughals, the emperor Akbar, had been discouraged from performing the Hajj with his aunt Gulbadan, and other female relatives on account of length and danger of the journey. We can see the problematic situations during that period and Sikander breaking the wall suggests her courage to stay away from the rituals undergoing. Yet only Hajj was obligatory, a point that reflects on issues of motivation, as well as perceptions of 'centre' and 'periphery' within the Islamic world. Writing a Muslim journey in a colonial environment shows the way for formation of identity. The research also justifies how her travelogue can be considered as semi-autobiography. The way she portrays the whole scenario doesn't hold any connection with the title too. Hence, we can say that the title is misleading but not in a negative way. But the circumstances in which she wrote was demanding a title like to this to continue during that era. Both the writers intended to British audience as well. They took very crucial topics during that period. New topics, defining the Self against others hold very sensitive topic. Spiritual quest is different from the quest of identity. We can nowhere see the soul-searching rather we will find things that in a way helps society to grow up.

In the annals of travel literature, the voices of women have often been reduced to whispers, their narratives overshadowed by the bold proclamations of empire, masculinity, and conquest. Yet when we pause, really pause, and tune into the travelogues of women like Nawab Sikander Begum and Fanny Parkes, we hear something astonishing—a layered symphony of insight, emotion, resistance, curiosity, and power. These are not mere accounts of where the authors have been. They are chronicles of becoming, meditations on the self in motion, on identity both fixed and fluid, and on what it means to see and be seen in a world structured by gender, race, and imperial authority.

This book has endeavoured to place two remarkable women writers—separated by geography, faith, and social position—into dialogue. And in doing so, it has revealed how travel writing becomes a vessel not only for documenting the world, but also for claiming one's place within it. Nawab Sikander Begum and Fanny Parkes, through their distinctly different journeys, both literal and metaphorical, challenge the dominant narratives of their time. Their works invite us to rethink the boundaries between public and private, domestic and political, observer and participant.

Throughout history, travel has been tethered to privilege—of wealth, class, mobility, and above all, masculinity. For much of the pre-modern and colonial world, the freedom to traverse space was linked with the assumption of male entitlement. Women's movement, in contrast, was hemmed in by domesticity, chastity, and duty. A woman who travelled alone, or who wrote boldly of her encounters, was not just a rarity; she was often a transgressor. She violated societal expectations and defied the scripts written for her by religion, culture, and empire.

Yet this very act of transgression is what makes the travelogues of Nawab Sikander Begum and Fanny Parkes so revolutionary. Their writings are not confined to the act of describing a place. Rather, they reclaim space— physical, intellectual, emotional—and inscribe themselves into geographies from which women have historically been erased.

In *A Princess's Pilgrimage*, Sikander Begum traverses the deeply spiritual and historically male-dominated landscape of the Islamic Hajj. She does so not only as a devout Muslim, but as a ruler, a critic, and a modern woman deeply attuned to the need for reform—both spiritual and societal. Her observations on governance, sanitation, and gender relations in Mecca are informed by a unique positionality: she is both insider and outsider, Muslim and monarch, native and subject of empire. Her travel becomes an act of layered reclamation—not just of religious piety, but of political and narrative agency.

Fanny Parkes, in *Wanderings of a Pilgrim in Search of the Picturesque*, steps into the Indian subcontinent not with the detachment of a colonial bureaucrat's wife, but with a heart full of curiosity. She learns the language, walks through temples, meets with Indian women in their zenanas, and records not only what she sees but what she feels. Her travel, too, becomes reclamation: of voice, of perspective, and of an empathetic engagement that defies the typical colonial gaze. Even when entangled in orientalist assumptions, Parkes shows the possibility of a gaze that is not entirely domineering—a gaze that seeks to know, not just to define.

One of the central concerns of this study has been the search for identity through travel writing. Both Sikander Begum and Fanny Parkes engage in this search, albeit through different lenses. For Sikander, the journey to Mecca is both a reaffirmation of faith and a renegotiation of her public role. In critiquing the corrupt officials in Arabia and expressing her disappointment with certain social customs, she is, in effect, articulating a vision for Islamic modernity—one that blends religious devotion with rational governance, and tradition with progress. This vision, published in English and intended for a British-Indian audience, also marks her as a self-aware political actor navigating the complex terrain of colonial politics.

For Parkes, identity is forged through immersion. Her long stay in India allows her to shed, at least partially, the rigid categories of colonizer and subject. She becomes a hybrid figure, neither fully British nor fully Indian, but something in-between. Her identity, like her prose, is textured—sometimes contradictory, always searching. In her descriptions of festivals, her admiration for Indian women, and her detailed notes on local customs, Parkes constructs a self that is shaped by cultural encounter. She does not merely observe India; she absorbs it, and in doing so, redefines herself.

This transformation of identity through travel is not accidental. Movement destabilizes certainty. It exposes one to the unfamiliar, challenges preconceived notions, and forces the traveller to ask: Who am I in relation to this world I am moving through? Both Sikander and Parkes grapple with this question—not always explicitly, but through the very act of writing their journeys. Their travelogues are diaries of self-invention, places where womanhood, power, spirituality, and intellect converge.

In colonial travel writing, the gaze—the way the observer views the observed—has historically been a mechanism of control. The imperial gaze sought to document, categorize, and dominate the colonized world. It rendered the subject passive, exotic, and often inferior. Women, both European and native, were doubly marginalized within this structure. They were seen and spoken for, rather than being allowed to see and speak.

Yet the travelogues of Parkes and Sikander invert this gaze. They do not simply look outward; they also reflect inward. Their gaze is not just about dominion—it is about interpretation, empathy, and critique. Sikander's gaze is at once devout and diagnostic. When she criticizes the inefficiency of Arabian administration or expresses shock at unsanitary conditions, she is not exoticizing the Arab world; she is positioning herself as a reformer. Her gaze is that of a ruler, a woman of vision, a subject with the capacity to judge, not merely to be judged.

Parkes' gaze, while at times imbued with orientalist romanticism, is softened by affection and curiosity. She observes not to dominate but to understand. Her entries brim with sensory detail, personal reaction, and genuine admiration. In her descriptions of Hindu festivals or Indian art, one senses a woman who is deeply moved by what she sees—even when she cannot fully comprehend it. She, too, rewrites the gaze: from an instrument of power to a lens of connection.

If travel allowed these women to move physically and intellectually, writing allowed them to move socially and politically. Authorship was, and remains, a form of power. To write is to inscribe oneself into history, to claim a voice, to resist erasure. For women in the 19th century, this was no small feat. Publishing a travelogue was not simply about narrating an adventure—it was about stepping into the public sphere, asserting intellectual authority, and demanding to be heard.

Sikander Begum's decision to publish her Hajj account in English, through the help of a British confidante, was both strategic and symbolic. It allowed her to reach an audience far beyond her own cultural or religious community. It placed her narrative alongside those of explorers, administrators, and reformers—almost all of them men. And it asserted, with quiet dignity, that a Muslim woman, a colonized princess, had something to say about the world, and that her words mattered.

Fanny Parkes, too, gained a kind of social capital through her writing. Her travelogue, along with the artefacts she brought home, granted her access to intellectual circles in Britain that might otherwise have been closed to her. Her experiences in India—filtered through her letters and journals—became the foundation of a new identity, one that defied the narrow confines of a colonial wife. Through her authorship, Parkes became not just a witness to history but a contributor to it.

In this way, the travelogues become more than

Echoes from the Margins | 155

texts; they become tools of empowerment. They give shape to experience and turn private journeys into public interventions.

This book has repeatedly returned to the idea that women's travel writing is not merely a variation on a male-dominated genre. It is, in many ways, its own tradition—a feminist act of seeing, moving, and narrating. The works of Sikander Begum and Fanny Parkes exemplify this tradition in rich and varied ways.

Both authors navigate structures of patriarchy and empire, but they do not do so passively. They critique, reinterpret, and sometimes repurpose these structures. Sikander, as a female Muslim monarch in a colonial world, reclaims Islamic modernity for women. Parkes, as a British expatriate in India, reclaims curiosity and emotional intelligence as tools of cultural engagement. Neither fits neatly into the roles assigned to them by history. And that is precisely their power.

Their legacy is not limited to the 19th century. It extends into our own time, where women's travel writing continues to challenge boundaries, redefine identity, and push back against hegemonic narratives. Contemporary writers—from Arundhati Roy to Elizabeth Gilbert, from Fatima Bhutto to Chimamanda Ngozi Adichie—owe a silent debt to pioneers like Parkes and Sikander, who showed that women's journeys, both literal and literary, matter.

In closing, the travelogues of Nawab Sikander Begum and Fanny Parkes offer us not only compelling stories of movement but profound meditations on power, perspective, and voice. Their journeys through physical landscapes mirror their inner journeys through faith, empire, womanhood, and authorship.

In *A Princess's Pilgrimage*, we encounter a woman

who is as much a stateswoman as a pilgrim. In *Wanderings of a Pilgrim*, we find a traveller who is both colonizer and empathizer, outsider and enthusiast. Their narratives complicate the binaries of East and West, colonizer and colonized, woman and writer.

To study their work is to encounter history not as a sequence of dates and events, but as a collage of lived experience—messy, beautiful, contradictory, and deeply human. It is to recognize that in every page of a travelogue written by a woman, there is an act of courage, a claiming of space, and a rewriting of what it means to know the world.

Their voices—sometimes humble, sometimes proud, always searching—resound across time. And in listening to them, we do more than recover lost histories. We enrich our present. We expand our understanding of what literature can do. And we honour the women who dared, quite simply, to go.

Moreover, what these two travelogues ultimately illuminate is that travel is never just a matter of geography—it is about transformation. For Nawab Sikander Begum and Fanny Parkes, to journey was to step out of the narrowly prescribed roles assigned to them as women and step into a space of self-definition. In Sikander Begum's case, the act of undertaking the Hajj, recording her impressions, and sharing them with a public—particularly a British-Indian one—was an act of multifaceted resistance. It was a claim to spiritual legitimacy, a challenge to colonial assumptions about Muslim women, and an assertion of her own political consciousness. Her critiques of the mismanagement in Mecca, her commentary on the condition of Arabian women, and her comparative reflections reveal a woman acutely aware of her complex positionality within intersecting axes of faith, gender, and empire. Likewise, Parkes' prolonged immersion in Indian culture, her attempts to understand the intricacies of domestic and religious life in the subcontinent, and her decision to document these experiences with openness, sincerity, and sometimes contradiction, demonstrate a kind of moral courage. These were not mere sightseeing tours; they were journeys that unsettled, challenged, and ultimately redefined the traveller herself. Through the act of travel and the equally significant act of writing, both women underwent transformations that reveal how the very process of movement can forge new selves—braver, more complex, and more whole.

In today's context, where conversations around postcolonialism, feminism and representation have evolved but remain unfinished, the writings of Sikander Begum and Fanny Parkes remain startlingly relevant. They speak to the ongoing need to foreground diverse voices and to examine how race, gender, and class shape the stories we tell about the world—and ourselves. Their travelogues offer not just windows into the past, but mirrors through which we can examine our present. Who gets to speak? Who gets to move freely across borders, physical or intellectual? Who gets to write the world into narrative form? In centring these two women, this study has sought not only to analyse literature, but to honour a tradition of female authorship that defies silencing. It reminds us that even within systems designed to marginalize, there are voices that refuse to be muted—voices that wander, witness, and write their way into the archive of history. These are the voices we must continue to read, teach, and elevate, because they remind us of the power of storytelling—not just as a record of what has been, but as a guide for what could be.

Works Cited

- Adams, Percy G. *Travel Literature and the Evolution of the Novel.* University Press of Kentucky, 1983.
- Ahmed-Ghosh, Huma. "Writing the Nation on the Beauty of the Nation: Women, Islam, and Representations of the Nation in Bangladesh." *Meridians*, vol. 4, no. 1, 2003, pp. 109–132. JSTOR, www.jstor.org/stable/40338615.
- Appiah, Kwame Anthony. *Cosmopolitanism: Ethics in a World of Strangers.* W.W. Norton, 2006.
- Birkett, Dea. "Spinsters Abroad." *Gender, Genre, and Identity in Women's Travel Writing,* edited by Kristi Siegel, Peter Lang, 2004, pp. 1–14.
- Blunt, Alison. *Travel, Gender, and Imperialism: Mary Kingsley and West Africa.* Guilford Press, 1994.
- Burton, Antoinette. *Dwelling in the Archive: Women Writing House, Home, and History in Late Colonial India.* Oxford University Press, 2003.
- Certeau, Michel de. *The Practice of Everyday Life.* Translated by Steven Rendall, University of California Press, 1984.
- Chakravarti, Uma. "Whatever Happened to the Vedic Dasi?" *Recasting Women: Essays in Colonial History,* edited by Kumkum Sangari and Sudesh Vaid, Rutgers University Press, 1990, pp. 27–87.

- Clifford, James. *Routes: Travel and Translation in the Late Twentieth Century*. Harvard University Press, 1997.
- Eco, Umberto. *Six Walks in the Fictional Woods*. Translated by Richard Dixon, Harvard University Press, 1994.
- Fanon, Frantz. *The Wretched of the Earth*. Translated by Richard Philcox, Grove Press, 2004.
- Foucault, Michel. *Power/Knowledge: Selected Interviews and Other Writings, 1972–1977*. Edited by Colin Gordon, Pantheon Books, 1980.
- Kaplan, Caren. *Questions of Travel: Postmodern Discourses of Displacement*. Duke University Press, 1996.
- Korte, Barbara. *English Travel Writing from Pilgrimages to Postcolonial Explorations*. Palgrave Macmillan, 2000.
- Lahiri, Jhumpa. *The Namesake*. Houghton Mifflin Harcourt, 2003.
- Mills, Sara. *Discourses of Difference: An Analysis of Women's Travel Writing and Colonialism*. Routledge, 1991.
- Parkes, Fanny. *Wanderings of a Pilgrim in Search of the Picturesque*. Edited by William Dalrymple, Oxford University Press, 2002.
- Parry, Benita. *Postcolonial Studies: A Materialist Critique*. Routledge, 2004.
- Porter, Roy. *Rewriting the Self: Histories from the Renaissance to the Present*. Routledge, 1997.
- Pratt, Mary Louise. *Imperial Eyes: Travel Writing and Transculturation*. Routledge, 1992.
- Rajan, Rajeswari Sunder. *Real and Imagined Women: Gender, Culture and Postcolonialism*. Routledge, 1993.
- Said, Edward W. *Orientalism*. Vintage Books, 1979.
- Sharpe, Jenny. *Allegories of Empire: The Figure of Woman in the Colonial Text*. University of Minnesota Press, 1993.
- Sikandar Begum, Nawab. *A Princess's Pilgrimage*. Translated by Antoinette Burton, Oxford University Press, 2007.

- Singh, Meera. *Voices Across Borders: Women's Journeys and Narrative Identity.* Oxford University Press, 2017.
- Spivak, Gayatri Chakravorty. "Can the Subaltern Speak?" *Marxism and the Interpretation of Culture,* edited by Cary Nelson and Lawrence Grossberg, University of Illinois Press, 1988, pp. 271–313.
- Thompson, Carl. *Travel Writing.* Routledge, 2011.
- Tucker, Herbert F. "The Moment of Postmodern Travel Writing." *Modern Philology,* vol. 91, no. 3, 1994, pp. 305–317.
- Young, Robert J.C. *Postcolonialism: An Historical Introduction.* Blackwell Publishing, 2001.

Black Eagle Books

www.blackeaglebooks.org
info@blackeaglebooks.org

Black Eagle Books, an independent publisher, was founded as a nonprofit organization in April, 2019. It is our mission to connect and engage the Indian diaspora and the world at large with the best of works of world literature published on a collaborative platform, with special emphasis on foregrounding Contemporary Classics and New Writing.

www.ingramcontent.com/pod-product-compliance
Lightning Source LLC
Chambersburg PA
CBHW060609080526
44585CB00013B/747